Magstræde
very old street

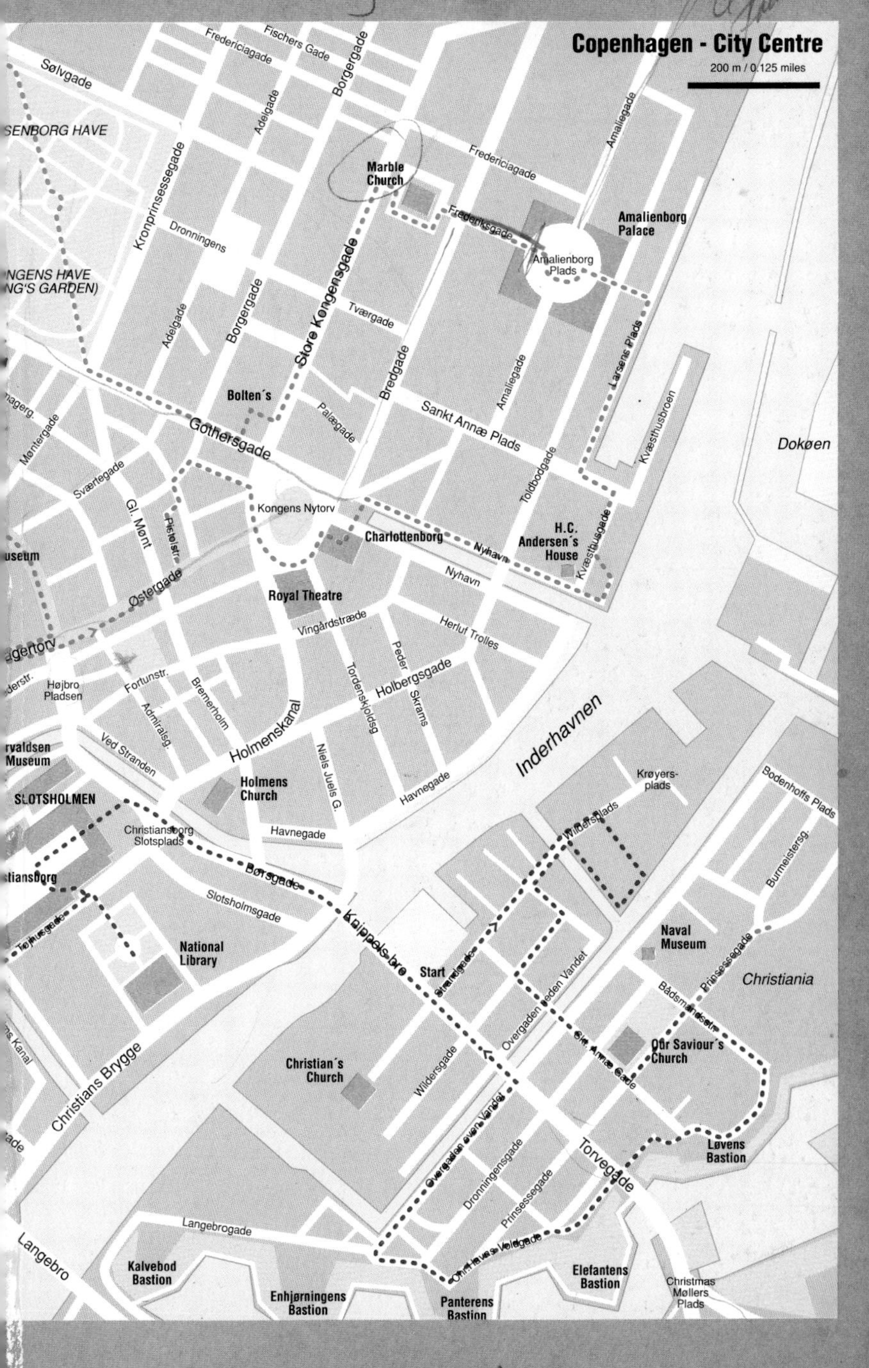

Kastrup

Amager

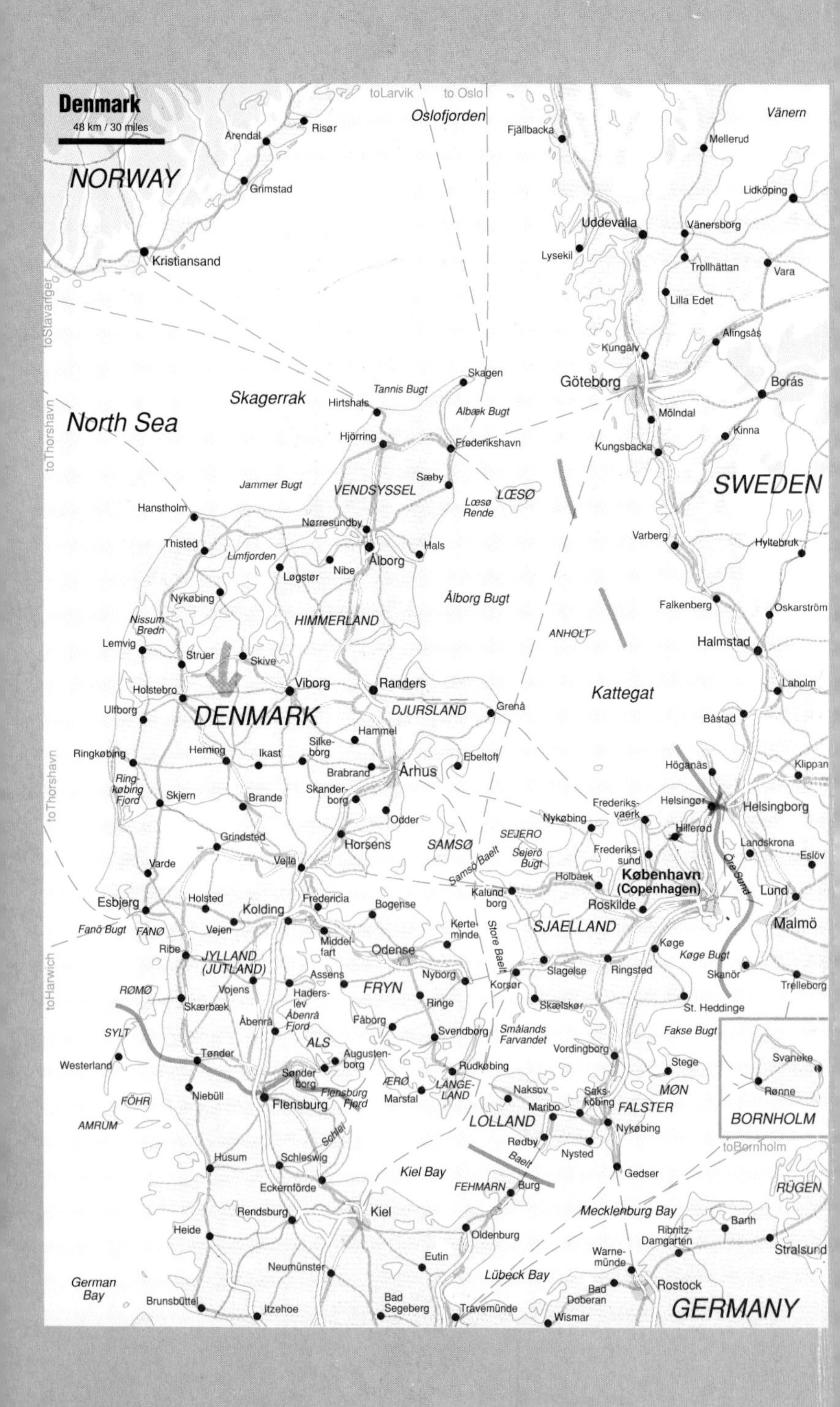

Denmark
48 km / 30 miles
NORWAY
Arendal
Risør
Grimstad
Kristiansand
to Larvik
to Oslo
Oslofjorden
Fjällbacka
Vänern
Mellerud
Lidköping
Uddevalla
Vänersborg
Lysekil
Trollhättan
Vara
Lilla Edet
Alingsås
Kungälv
to Stavanger
Skagerrak
Skagen
Göteborg
Borås
Tannis Bugt
Hirtshals
Albæk Bugt
Mölndal
North Sea
Kinna
Hjørring
Frederikshavn
Kungsbacka
to Thorshavn
Sæby
SWEDEN
Jammer Bugt
VENDSYSSEL
Læsø Rende
LÆSØ
Hanstholm
Nørresundby
Varberg
Hyltebruk
Thisted
Limfjorden
Hals
Ålborg
Nibe
Løgstør
Nykøbing
Ålborg Bugt
Falkenberg
Oskarström
Nissum Bredn
HIMMERLAND
ANHOLT
Halmstad
Lemvig
Struer
Skive
Viborg
Randers
Laholm
Holstebro
Kattegat
Ulfborg
DENMARK
DJURSLAND
Grenå
Båstad
Hammel
Ringkøbing
Herning
Ikast
Silkeborg
Ebeltoft
Höganäs
Klippan
Ring-købing Fjord
Brabrand
Århus
Skjern
Brande
Skanderborg
Frederiksvaerk
Helsingør
Helsingborg
Odder
Nykøbing
Hillerød
Grindsted
Horsens
SAMSØ
SEJERØ
Landskrona
Sejerø Bugt
Frederikssund
Eslöv
Varde
Vejle
Samsø Baelt
Holbaek
København (Copenhagen)
Öresund
Kalundborg
Lund
Esbjerg
Holsted
Kolding
Fredericia
Bogense
Roskilde
Fanø Bugt
FANØ
Vejen
Kerteminde
SJAELLAND
Malmö
Middelfart
Store Baelt
Ribe
JYLLAND (JUTLAND)
Odense
Køge
Køge Bugt
Assens
Nyborg
Slagelse
Ringsted
Skanör
Trelleborg
RØMØ
Vojens
Haderslev
FRYN
Korsør
Skærbæk
Ringe
Skælskør
St. Heddinge
Åbenrå
Åbenrå Fjord
Fåborg
Svendborg
Smålands Farvandet
Fakse Bugt
SYLT
ALS
Vordingborg
Westerland
Tønder
Augustenborg
Rudkøbing
Stege
Svaneke
Sønderborg
ÆRØ
LANGELAND
Naksov
Sakskøbing
MØN
Rønne
FÖHR
Niebüll
Flensburg
Flensburg Fjord
Marstal
Maribo
FALSTER
AMRUM
LOLLAND
Nykøbing
BORNHOLM
Schlei
Rødby
Nysted
to Bornholm
Husum
Schleswig
Baelt
Kiel Bay
Gedser
FEHMARN
Burg
RÜGEN
Eckernförde
Rendsburg
Kiel
Mecklenburg Bay
Barth
Heide
Oldenburg
Ribnitz-Damgarten
Warnemünde
Stralsund
Eutin
Neumünster
Lübeck Bay
Rostock
German Bay
Bad Doberan
Brunsbüttel
Itzehoe
Bad Segeberg
Travemünde
Wismar
GERMANY
to Harwich

INSIGHT POCKET GUIDES

Written and Presented by **Jo Hermann**

Jo Hermann

Robert Kreuse
31-556495

Insight Pocket Guide:

DENMARK

Directed by
Hans Höfer

Managing Editor
Andrew Eames

Photography by
Marianne Paul

Design Concept by
V. Barl

Design by
Frances Hinton

Printed in Singapore by
Höfer Press (Pte) Ltd
Fax: 65-8616438

Distributed in the United States by
Houghton Mifflin Company
222 Berkeley Street
Boston, Massachusetts 02116-3764
ISBN: 0-395-68229-0

Distributed in Canada by
Thomas Allen & Son
390 Steelcase Road East
Markham, Ontario L3R 1G2
ISBN: 0-395-68229-0

Distributed in the UK & Ireland by
GeoCenter International UK Ltd
The Viables Center, Harrow Way
Basingstoke, Hampshire RG22 4BJ
ISBN: 9-62421-565-0

Worldwide distribution enquiries:
Höfer Communications Pte Ltd
38 Joo Koon Road
Singapore 2262
ISBN: 9-62421-565-0

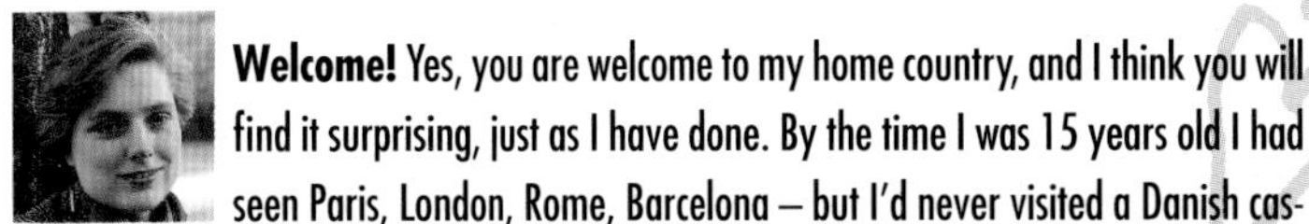

Welcome! Yes, you are welcome to my home country, and I think you will find it surprising, just as I have done. By the time I was 15 years old I had seen Paris, London, Rome, Barcelona – but I'd never visited a Danish castle or a manor house. My eyes were first opened to the wealth of history and landscape in my own country when I began to study architecture, and since then I've travelled the length and breadth of Denmark. For the last 10 years I've been working as a writer and editor – including three years in America – and while I have the knowledge of an insider for my own country, I also have the advantage of a foreigner's perspective.

In these pages I'm your personal guide, and for you I've created tailormade itineraries to the best of Denmark, dividing the country into its best sections: Copenhagen and Surroundings, Århus and Around and North Jutland. These sections then have their own full-day and half-day tours and excursions, into which I've crammed a whole range of sites and activities. Designer shopping, trips to Sweden, Hamlet's castle, the Tivoli Gardens, the liberal community of Christiania, sand dunes that move, neolithic monuments, Viking tombs – all and more are here. And wherever I take you I ensure that you will know exactly where to rest and where to eat.

In the back of the book I've recommended restaurants, nightlife and the year's most exciting events. I've also prepared all the practical information that you could need.

Hygge is a key word in Denmark; in summer, *hygge* might be to go to an outdoor concert, or to drink a few beers in good company. You can also *hygge* yourself with a good book and a warm blanket. *Hygge* cannot be bought or sold; it arises from a feeling of being at ease, and I hope you'll experience some *hyggelige* hours while you're here.

Welcome! Velkommen! — Jo Hermann

Contents

Preceding pages: superb cycling country

Maps

***Following pages:* opera fans in Copenhagen**

Denmark's present border was established as late as 1920, when the people of Slesvig voted on whether they wanted to live on the Danish or the German side of the border. The result of this vote was that Northern Slesvig 'came home' to Denmark, while the southern part of the old duchy preferred to unite with Germany. This partitioning was the culmination of 1700 years of strife, war and migration during which the Danes had alternately tried to control other countries and struggled to survive as a nation. I will try to make a long story short.

Grave Mounds are still visible

The Beginning

The first people to set foot in Jutland some 240,000 years ago were pre-Neanderthals who were hunting reindeer. But the ice forced them away again. The first hunters who stayed didn't arrive until around 12,000BC. Deep dark woods covered the country then, but around 4200BC something happened: a new group of people moved in, the first farmers. They began to burn the trees and cultivate the land and in the ground they found flint, a prime material for axes and sharp tools. The farmers buried their dead in grave mounds, some of which are still visible in today's landscape.

Around 1800BC traders from the south introduced bronze, and new wealth reached the country. The metal came from south-east Europe and was traded for amber, cattle and fur. Around 500BC, when iron replaced bronze, the picture changed again. Iron was harder and could be produced locally, and made it possible for the farmers to develop new tools and more efficient techniques. Cultivated land slowly began to replace the woods. The country was becoming more populous, and people began to fight each other for land. Around 250BC a number of tribes from North Jutland, among them the Cimbres, the Teutons and the Vandals, began to migrate towards the south.

The next wave of migration came north. Around 200AD, the Danes left North Germany to settle in Scania (South Sweden) and on Zealand, where they drove out the original population. 300 years later, they had taken Jutland as well and *Danmark* had come into being.

Viking Ship

The Vikings

In the second half of the 8th century, the Scandinavians designed a new kind of boat: a long, slim and slightly arched vessel that could come ashore at just about any type of coast. And it did. The Vikings soon became feared from Italy to Greenland and from Ireland to Russia. The different nations all participated in the pillaging: in general, the Norwegian Vikings stayed in the north, while the Swedes went east, and the Danes took care of England and Western Europe.

The Viking Age is often counted from

Golden Horns, Viking era

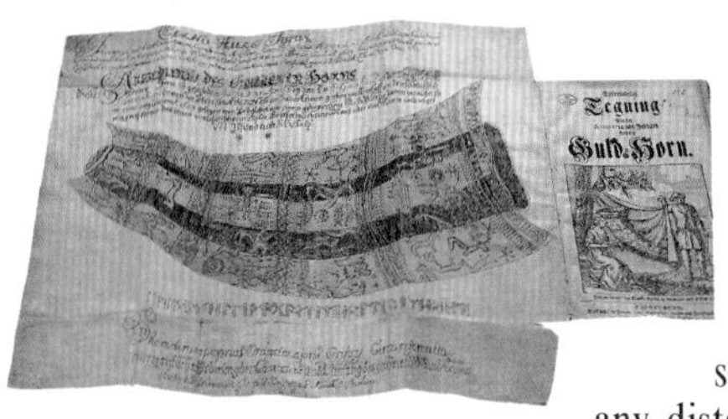

793, when the monks at Lindisfarne in Northumberland were the first to receive uninvited guests from the north. Until then, people had considered it impossible to travel any distance on the high seas; but the Vikings could go much farther than this. In 806 the Danes attacked Ireland; in 810 the Frisians received a visit; in 843 Danish Vikings sailed up the river Loire to Nantes, and the following year they scared the Moors in Spain; in 845 Paris paid a ransom in order not to be attacked, but another group of Vikings hit them later; and around 900 Normandy became a Danish Viking colony. The Danes ruled in north-east England from 871, and they kept fighting until king Canute (Knud in Danish) had gained power over the entire country in 1016. They where forced back in 1066, when William the Conqueror won the Battle of Hastings and occupied England. Another Danish prince Knud returned to try to regain England a decade later, but without success. After three centuries, the Viking Age was finally over, and Denmark began to shrink again.

The Vikings didn't listen to prayers, didn't feel obliged to keep their promises, didn't shy away from sly tricks and even attacked other Viking countries. Still they were not quite as barbaric as legend has it. Some historians even maintain that they were welcomed by the British women, because they washed themselves on a regular basis. But the best evidence of their level of cultural achievement was in their villages. We know four of them, all extremely well-organized: Trelleborg on West Zealand, Nonnebakken on Funen, Fyrkat in Hobro in central Jutland, and Aggersborg close to Limfjorden in North Jutland. The houses are laid out along straight lines, either radiating from the centre or in square blocks across two axes, with a circular rampart to protect each village. These villages show that the Vikings must have been skilled in geometry – the same

Building in Stone

In the 12th century the Danes learned to build in stone and tile. Although this new technique was too expensive to apply to ordinary houses, it was not so for God's house. In the 12th century alone, 2,000 communities erected stone churches, most of which are still standing. They were built in either the heavy Romanesque style or the more elegant Gothic style and richly decorated with frescoes. Church towers were not yet in fashion at the time of building, but were added later. At the time of the Reformation, the churches were whitewashed to erase all traces of their Catholic past, but many of the frescoes have since been recovered.

The aristocracy also built their houses in stone. Since farming was the main source of income for both rich and poor, most of the manor houses were built in the country. They reflect the style of their time (and the wallet of the builder) and range from large farm houses to castles with towers and moats, to elegant palaces. The churches and manor houses are a real architectural treasure, unique to Denmark.

Church fresco detail

knowledge which enabled them to travel all over Europe without losing their way.

A Christian Nation

Gorm den Gamle (Old Gorm) was the first king to rule over the country called Denmark, and the members of the royal family descend from this old man.

Before the 900s, the country had been inhabited by tribes who regarded themselves as neighbours and kinsmen, but felt no need to organise themselves under one ruler. Matters were settled locally, but attacks from Swedish Vikings and general unrest in the early 900s paved the road for a strong man to take command. Hardeknud was the one who threw out the Swedes, and thereby he gained a position of power for himself. His son Gorm became the first king of Denmark; we know him best from the rune-stone his son set in the small East Jutland town of Jelling in memory of his parents: 'King Harald bade to make these runes after Gorm, his father, and Thyra, his mother, the Harald who won all of Denmark and Norway and made the Danes Christian.'

During the next three centuries Denmark was constantly engaged in war, even after the Viking Age had ended. Germany was the main target, because the Germans controlled most of the trade in the Baltic region. In 1397, Denmark, Norway and Sweden finally teamed up to drive out the Germans, who had occupied a good part of Jutland and Sweden, Stockholm included. The union was spearheaded by Queen Margrethe I, who eventually became the ruler of all three countries. But the notion of brotherhood between the Scandinavians never really caught on; the Swedes pulled out, and years of exhausting wars with Germany and Sweden followed.

Meanwhile, the revolutionary theses of Martin Luther had reached Copenhagen. In 1536, King Christian III jumped on this chance to wrestle power and possessions from the hands of the Catholic church – realising that this was really the only way to pay the huge national debt the wars had incurred. Thus it was that Denmark became a Lutheran country.

Around the end of the 16th century, Christian IV entered the scene as the most enterprising king Denmark has ever had. He had a keen interest in architecture, music, ship-

King Christian III

Christian IV's Rosenborg Castle

building, trade, farming, warfare, you name it. He wouldn't leave it to his secretary to write his letters, and he wouldn't leave it to the architects to design his buildings. He was directly responsible for the design of the Round Tower, Rosenborg Castle and many others in Copenhagen. Unfortunately, he was just as convinced about his abilities as a general, and he engaged in new wars with Sweden that continued long after his death. The country was once again in debt, and as the aristocracy refused to pay its share, so the heaviest burden fell on the merchants. They responded by supporting the monarchy against the aristocracy. At a quiet revolution in 1660, King Frederik III was given absolute power.

During the reign of the enterprising Christian IV, Denmark had founded its first colony Trankebar in Ceylon, and the colonial trade grew rapidly. Throughout the 18th century, Danish merchants made huge profits from such trade. Wars between the English and the French had the effect of cutting France off from its colonies, and Denmark jumped at the chance to sell its own colonial produce to France. The British were not amused, and in 1801 they sent Lord Nelson to Copenhagen, where he defeated a haphazardly-gathered fleet of floats and worn-out battle ships. Six years later, when Denmark had sided with Napoleon, the British came back and bombed the city back into poverty. The fire lasted three days and when it was over, the British navy sailed away with what was left of the fleet.

Hans Christian Andersen

Economically Denmark was on its knees, but culturally the country was going through one of its most prolific periods ever. Hans Christian Andersen wrote his fairy tales and novels, while Søren Kierkegaard pondered the essential questions of being, and in Rome a host of painters and sculptors gathered around Bertel Thorvaldsen, who sold his classical marble statues all over Europe. August Bournonville studied in Paris, but came back to Copenhagen to introduce his new techniques at the Royal Ballet. Hans Christian Ørsted discovered the electro-magnetic field, and Rasmus Rask found the first traces of the Indo-European language. It was a golden age at a low budget.

The Coming of Democracy

Inspired by the French revolutions, Danish liberals demanded a new constitution in 1848. Since the government wouldn't listen, the citizens went straight to the king, who would. It took another year to work out the specifics of the constitution and 50 years of feuds between the two chambers the Rigsdagen and the Folketinget to implement it. The aristocracy of the Rigsdagen simply issued provisionary emergency laws so that it could have its own way. But while the aristocracy ruled, the people proved that they were quite capable of handling their own affairs. The farmers organised dairy co-ops, where one man had one vote, no matter if he had 10 or 30 cows. They also sought to improve their skills at the high schools which the visionary priest Grundtvig had started for people of little or no education. In 1901, the farmers finally got a chance to govern the country.

The farmers had their co-operatives and the workers their unions. Meanwhile in the cities, the Social Democratic Party had been growing, and in 1924 it was their turn to form a government. Tobacco worker Thorvald Stauning became prime minister and stayed in power with only one interruption until his death in 1942.

Germans advance in Denmark in 1940

During this period, the country went a long way down the road towards social democracy. The first step was to pass new social laws and give benefits to unemployed workers. Since 1933, begging has become a thing of the past – Denmark believes that the needy have a right to be helped.

When the Germans invaded Denmark on their way to Norway in 1940, Stauning decided not to fight. He thought that Denmark should be under German 'protection' until the war was over, but that meanwhile it could remain an independent nation. Politicians from all parties joined in a new coalition behind this principle. But some people didn't agree. The resistance movement kept growing, and after a general strike in 1943, the government resigned and the Germans took over. Later the same year, the Germans decided to deport the Danish Jews, but they only managed to round up 500 people; members of the resistance movement had helped another 6,500 across the sound to Sweden.

Margrethe II became Queen of Denmark in 1972

Denmark had fully recovered from the war by the beginning of the 1960s and experienced tremendous growth thereafter. The Social Democrats had set the agenda: The new wealth should reach everybody. Thus, the standard of living for ordinary people was elevated to one of the highest levels in the world. But the money was, to a large extent, borrowed and the worldwide oil crisis in 1973 hit hard. Inflation was high and the debt just kept growing. During the 1980s, leading politicians began to talk about national bankruptcy as a realistic possibility. Denmark was 'going to Hell in First Class'.

The Social Democrats wanted some breathing space and so they resigned, hoping to come back to power with the right solution. Meanwhile Poul Schlüter from the Conservative Party had assumed office, and he had no intention of giving it away. It was his ambition to change the agenda, and so he did: privatisation of public institutions, cuts in public spending and tax breaks for export companies was the medicine that he considered should bring Denmark back on track. He celebrated his 10th anniversary in 1992, and has in fact managed to pay off huge chunks of the national debt. The major cost has been a rise in unemployment.

Denmark has been a full member of the EC since 1972, but nevertheless turned down the resolutions of the Maastricht treaty in 1992 – much to the surprise of everybody, even the majority who said 'no'!

Historical Highlights

12000BC The first hunters arrive.
4200–1800 The Stone Age. Tools are made of flint and ceramics.
1800–500 The Bronze Age. Trade with the rest of Europe..
500BC–AD1000 The Iron Age. Farming develops.
300 First traces of battles between tribes on Danish ground.
AD200 The Danes settle on the islands and later in Jutland.
800–1050 The Viking Age. Vikings plunder Europe.
960 King Harald Bluetooth is christened. During his reign Denmark becomes one nation.
12th century About 2,000 stone churches are built.
1200 A new market for herring in Scania attracts traders far and wide.
1219 King Valdemar II conquers Estonia. For a short while, he controls the whole coastline from South Jutland to Estonia.
1397 Denmark unites with Norway and Sweden in the Kalmar Union, ruled by Margrethe I.
1536 The Reformation. Denmark becomes a Lutheran country.
1596–1648 Christian IV rules.
1640–1720 80 years of wars with Sweden.
1660 Absolute monarchy is introduced with Frederik III.
1728 & 1795 Fires ravage Copenhagen.
1733–88 Due to shortage of labourers in the country, farmers are denied the right to move away from their home districts.
1801 The British admiral Nelson defeats the Danes in a naval battle at Copenhagen, caused by a conflict of interest in the colonial trade.
1807 England forces Denmark out of its neutrality in the Napoleonic wars, then bombs Copenhagen and destroys the Danish fleet.
1813 Denmark declares national bankruptcy.
1814 Denmark's allegiance to Napoleon means that the country suffers reparations after Napoleon's defeat – and loses Norway.
1830 Recovering from the war, the people demand a voice in the administration of the country.
1835 The first fairy tales by Hans Christian Andersen are published.
1848 Christian VII dies. 15,000 citizens march to the new king Frederik VII to demand a constitution. When they arrive the government has already resigned.
1864 Denmark loses Slesvig-Holstein to Germany in a bloody battle.
1866–1901 The aristocracy rules assisted by provisionary emergency laws.
1901 The aristocracy resigns, and the constitution is finally effective.
1913 Niels Bohr presents his quantum theory.
1915 Women and servants achieve the right to vote.
1920 Parts of Slesvig are won back in a peaceful settlement.
1920 King Christian X dissolves the government, but is reproved by his people.
1924 The Social Democrats form their first government.
1933 Social reforms guarantee all citizens the right to unemployment benefits and state-funded pensions.
1940–45 Denmark is occupied by Germany.
1949 Denmark joins NATO.
1953 Due to a revision of the constitution, princess Margrethe becomes heir to the throne; the Rigsdagen is abolished.
1972 Denmark joins the EC.
1982 Conservative prime minister Poul Schlüter begins to transform social democratic Denmark, mainly by cutting public spending and privatising public institutions.
1992 Danes refuse to ratify the Maastricht treaty.

Copenhagen & Surroundings

Day 1

From Havn to København

The heart of Copenhagen: a day-long route that takes in Strøget, Nyhavn, Amalienborg Palace, Rosenborg Castle, Rundetårn, Helligåndskirken, the National Museum, Larsbjørnsstræde, Gråbrødre Torv, with shopping, coffee and lunch along the way. Evening at Café Sommersko.

–Starting point: Rådhuspladsen (The Town Hall Square), close to the central train station and on the route of most city buses. Buy a money-saving Copenhagen Card (CC) at the tourist information office between Tivoli and the train station. The changing of the guards at Amalienborg Palace takes place at noon; if you start around 9am, you should have plenty of time to get there. From mid-June to mid-September, the city tourist minibuses stop at most of the sights on this itinerary.–

In 1962, Copenhagen closed its central shopping street to traffic and turned it into a pedestrian street 1.1km (0.6 miles) long. All kinds of people have taken **Strøget** to heart. Shoppers, street vendors, musicians, jugglers, chess players and tourists rub elbows with political crusaders and busy office workers, so the street is often crowded and rarely boring. But if you

***Left:* Strøget juggler**

Copenhagen and Christiansborg Palace

get up early, you'll soon discover that most people don't. The majority of the shops don't open until 10am, and you'll have the opportunity to see the city come alive.

The first 250m (800ft) of Strøget covers the area where the original Viking hamlet of Havn was situated. The place was also known as Købmændenes Havn (The Merchants' Harbour) or, in short, København – the name still in use. Protected by the island of Amager, Havn provided a safe hiding place where pirates could be kept at a distance.

In 1167, King Valdemar gave Havn to his foster brother Absalon, who was the bishop of Roskilde, and he built his castle on an islet between Havn and Amager. He also extended the size of the hamlet considerably by building a rampart around the area from Rådhuspladsen to Kongens Nytorv (the full length of Strøget) and from his castle to Nørreport. This area is also known as the medieval city, and even today, it is still the heart of Copenhagen. The city has had a long history of wars and fires, and consequently very few buildings are left from that period, but the layout of the streets has remained almost the same as in those early days.

On Strøget

The first open space you'll come to is actually two squares: **Gammel Torv** and **Nytorv** (Old and New Square). Until the last big fire in 1795, they were separated by a town hall, but today they appear as one. In the centre of Gammel Torv stands the **Karitasbrønden** (Well of Charity), which was built in 1610. It was given to the people as a public well by the avid builder-king Christian IV. The well has been dramatically altered by later generations, who elevated the original figures, added a new foundation and called it a

Strøget

fountain. But one tradition persists: at royal birthdays, it cascades with 'golden' apples balanced on top of the water jets.

Walk on down Strøget to **Amagertorv** with Storkespringvandet (the Stork Fountain) and some of the best and most expensive shops in Copenhagen (we'll get back to that). If you look to the right, you'll see Christiansborg (the Parliament building) behind Højbro Square. Turn left two blocks further down Strøget into the passage named **Pistolstræde** (yes, Pistol Street, so called because of its shape). A century ago, this was the worst slum area in the city, but nowadays it is downright chic. If you skipped breakfast this morning, you can make up for it by tucking in at the bakery and café **Konditoriet** here.

When you get to the square where the pistol handle starts, there's a passage leading out into **Grønnegade**. Here, the City Museum has made a permanent exhibit of three old shop facades: a barber, a lingerie shop and an old-fashioned grocery store. Two doors to your left in Grønnegade, you'll find a modern shop selling copies of jewellery made during the Bronze, Iron and Viking Ages. When you've taken a look at that, walk the other way across Ny Østergade. The first street to your right will be Ny Adelgade, where Tage Andersen has his trend-setting flower shop. His dramatic creations made of fresh and dried flowers and branches in metal containers have added new life to many a dull window sill. You'll also find Galleri Asbæk here (a place to return to if you are fond of modern art; open Monday–Friday 11am–6pm, Saturday 11am–4pm).

Ny Adelgade leads up to **Kongens Nytorv** (the King's New Square). The king in question was Frederik III, successor to Christian IV. Frederik ordered several new squares to be built as part of a grander scheme to modernise Copenhagen, among them Kongens Nytorv. If you walk to the right, you'll find the grand Hotel d'Angleterre in the first of the mansions. Further up to the right is the depart-

Guarding Amalienborg Palace

ment store Magasin du Nord, and across the street lies **The Royal Theatre** – closed during the summer but try to peek through the glass doors. Continue to the brown brick mansion of **Charlottenborg**, home of the Academy of Fine Arts. To reach the exhibition building in the back you must walk through the two courtyards. In the hallway are bulletin boards with posters from art galleries all around the city and country, so this is the place for a quick overview of the best of the current shows.

Kongens Nytorv

When you leave, take the exit to the right, and you'll be standing on the bank of **Nyhavn Canal** (New Harbour). It used to be that Nyhavn had a nice and a naughty side. You are standing on the nice side. A few tattoo shops across the water still tell the story of what Nyhavn once was, but today, it is simply a charming restaurant strip and a nice place to stop, whether you are ready for lunch or just for a cup of coffee.

During the summer, tour boats leave from Nyhavn for a wonderful 50-minute cruise of the harbour area (Havnerundfarten, Tel: 33 13 31 05; May–mid-September: every 30 minutes, 10.15am-4.45pm; adults 36 kr., children 16 kr.). This is one of the least expensive and most memorable sightseeing tours in the city, and you should do it particularly if the weather is fine.

Back on land again, walk along the restaurant side of Nyhavn and follow the waterfront around the corner and past the Oslo boat until you come to the park, **Amaliehaven**. The Queen of Denmark resides at the **Amalienborg Palace** behind the fountain. At noon, fresh guardsmen come in to replace their tired colleagues. How many soldiers you'll get to see in this changing of the guards depends on how many members of the royal families are in town. When they have taken off for their summer residences, the show is somewhat less spectacular, but the place is still impressive. The statue in the centre of the square depicts Frederik V, who designed the palace in 1749. It is one of the finest equestrian statues in the world, and small wonder – it took the French sculptor Saly 20 years to finish it.

Behind the palace lies **Marmorkirken** (the Marble Church), easily recognisable by its huge cupola. The statues around it portray some of the greatest Danish names in religious philosophy, among them Søren Kierkegaard and N.F.S. Grundtvig, who founded the folk high schools (see the History section) and wrote the words for many of the hymns in the Danish song book. Store Kongensgade runs be-

Nyhavn Canal for cafés and restaurants

hind the church. Make a left turn along it and walk back towards Kongens Nytorv. Shortly before you get to the square, look for the **Bolten's** sign to the right. If you need to rest your legs, there are plenty of options in this little complex of restaurants and cafés; a good place for lunch. At the back end of Bolten's, you'll come out onto Gothersgade.

Turn right and follow the street to the first traffic lights. In front of you **Kongens Have** (the King's Garden) opens up, also known as Rosenborg Have after the castle it leads up to. Follow the path to the fountain and continue to the other end of the park. To get to the castle, you'll have to exit the park, turn left onto Nørre Voldgade and find the entrance from the street (June–August: daily 10am–4pm; May, September–21 October: daily 11am–3pm; 22 October–30 April: Tuesday, Friday and Sunday 11am–2pm; there's no electric light in the castle!).

Rosenborg was one of Christian IV's many projects, and he designed a good part of it himself. It was originally planned as the summer residence of the royal family, just outside the city, and three generations of kings have spent time there. But as the city grew, the royal family decided to move their 'summerhouse' out to Frederiksberg.

Rosenborg has been a museum since 1838, and it was one of the first of its kind to be arranged chronologically. The first three rooms you'll see were used by Christian IV, the next one by his successor Frederik III and so forth. The last king to be represented is Frederik VII, who in 1849 signed Denmark's first democratic constitution, then happily declared that from now on, he'd sleep late in the morning. In room 3, you'll find a true rarity: the clothes Christian IV was wearing during a battle with the Germans in which his eye was pierced. The bloodstains are still visible on the collar and the handkerchief. But apart from this curious piece,

The Marble Church

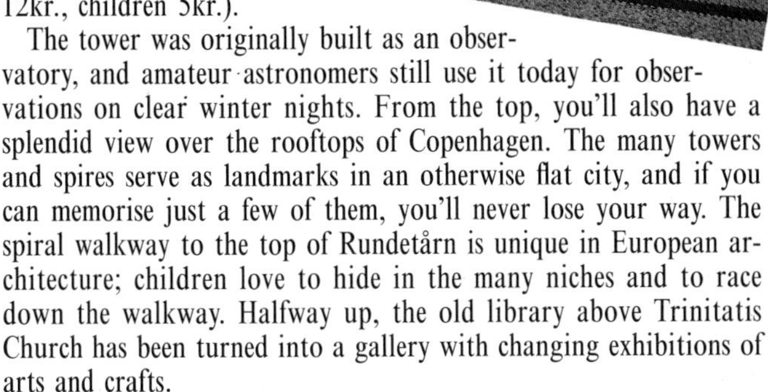

Rosenborg also presents marvellous treasures of furniture, paintings and tableware and, of course, the royal crown jewels.

When you leave the castle, turn left and walk the 500m up to the pedestrian street **Købmagergade**. About 300m up Købmagergade you'll come to another of Christian IV's buildings, **Rundetårn** (the Round Tower, June–August: daily 10am–8pm; April, May, September, October: Monday–Saturday 10am–5pm, Sunday noon–4pm; November–March: Monday–Saturday 10am–4pm, Sunday noon–4pm; adults 12kr., children 5kr.).

The tower was originally built as an observatory, and amateur astronomers still use it today for observations on clear winter nights. From the top, you'll also have a splendid view over the rooftops of Copenhagen. The many towers and spires serve as landmarks in an otherwise flat city, and if you can memorise just a few of them, you'll never lose your way. The spiral walkway to the top of Rundetårn is unique in European architecture; children love to hide in the many niches and to race down the walkway. Halfway up, the old library above Trinitatis Church has been turned into a gallery with changing exhibitions of arts and crafts.

Down again, turn left and walk back to Strøget for a bit of window-shopping. On Amagertorv you'll find three of the most exquisite shops in Copenhagen gathered within one block. Start with the silverware in **Georg Jensen**, then work your way through

Working in Kongens Have

Rundetårn's spiral walkway

the **Royal Copenhagen Porcelain** shop to **Illum's Bolighus** to look at modern design (I recommend you read the chapter on shopping in this book, before you start buying). The stores are all owned by the united breweries of Tuborg and Carlsberg, who have always had a strong interest in the arts.

If you follow Strøget back the way you came this morning, you'll soon come to **Helligåndskirken** (Church of the Holy Ghost). The church interior dates from the late 19th century, but the adjacent building to the left goes all the way back to the 15th century, when it was built by a religious order to function as a hospital for the poor.

Look for the passage called Klostergården across from the church. The peace and silence in this 1920s archway is a striking contrast to the noise of Strøget. It leads to Læderstræde, where the better end of Copenhagen's antique and carpet shops are located. Follow Naboløs down to Gammel Strand, and you'll be standing on the old shore-line facing Slotsholmen, where Absalon built his (long gone) castle. The narrow street to your right, **Snaregade**, is one of the oldest in the city. Several of the houses are from the 16th century and survived the fire of 1728. If you can get into No 4 (ask a resident), you'll see all the owners of the houses on this particular lot from 1397 to 1912 depicted on the walls.

When you reach Rådhusstræde, turn left, follow Frederiksholms Kanal and turn right at Ny Vestergade. Half way down the street stands the **National Museum** (5 June–15 September: daily 10am–5pm; 16 September–4 June: Monday–Friday 11am-3pm, weekends noon–4pm; adults 20 kr., children free). Buy your ticket, head back towards the entrance and make a left turn. That will take you to the old Danish collection. To get the chronology right, walk all the way down through the glass-covered walkway to the rune-stone hall and turn right. All signs are written in both English and Danish, and you can easily spend an hour studying the

Bohemian Larsbjørnstræde

collections. However, if you want only the highlights and haven't got much time, you should disregard the chronology, turn left from the room with the lur trumpets and just go through the Bronze Age and Viking collections. The runestone hall will then signal the end of the trip. But don't forget to take a look at the eerie room next to the lurs, where four people lie in their hollow oak coffins, the way they were buried in a peat bog ages ago.

Walk back the way you came through Rådhusstræde across Gammel Torv. The third street on your left will be Skt. Pedersstræde with **Skt. Petri Church** on the corner (three stops with bus No 5 will take you there as well). Although partly rebuilt, this is the oldest church in central Copenhagen with a chapel that dates back to the 13th century. The church belongs to the German congregation, and unfortunately you can only see it from the outside. Turn left, and you'll enter the bohemian neighbourhood of **Larsbjørnstræde**, usually at its most active in the late afternoon, which is about the time you should be there if you've followed this itinerary. This is the place to buy second-hand clothes, ecological vegetables, Indian jewellery, old comic books and the like, or just to hang out and watch people go by.

When you have tired of that, follow Vestergade back towards Gammel Torv and continue almost to the end of the street, where **Gråbrødre Torv** lies to your right. The Franciscan monks (the Greyfriars who gave the square its name) built their monastery here in the 13th century, but times have changed. Today, it is more like Nyhavn without the water. For your evening's leisure you can pick and choose among the restaurants and bars (**Peder Oxe** is always a safe bet), or if the weather's fine just enjoy a cool bottle of beer in the shade of the old plane tree.

Royal ironwork

If you find prices too stiff (or if you'd like a cup of coffee after dinner), walk across the square to Løvstræde, turn right at Købmagergade and left at the second street, Kronprinsensgade, home of **Café Sommersko**. Sommersko was the first real café in Denmark, and it is still among the liveliest at night. I like it here; maybe we'll run into each other one evening.

Christianshavn, Government and Gardens

Christianshavn with its canals and the free community of Christiania, the government, Christiansborg Castle, art museum Ny Carlsberg Glyptotek and dinner in the famous Tivoli Gardens (see map on pages IFC–1 for route).

Nautical but nice

–Make reservations for dinner in Tivoli (see below). Take bus No 2 or 8 from Rådhuspladsen or No 9 from Kongens Nytorv to the first stop in Christianshavn.–

Would you like to live in a quiet, yet lively traditional neighbourhood that is centrally located, has little traffic in the side streets, large park areas, a waterfront promenade and a canal with sailing boats, plus a good number of restaurants and bars? Well, now you know why it is difficult to find an apartment in Christianshavn.

Christian IV planned Christianshavn in 1618 as part of his line of defence around Copenhagen. It started out as a naval base, and until a few years ago the navy still had its quarters at Holmen on the north-east side of Christianshavn. If you walk along **Strandgade**, the front street facing the city, you'll find many houses from the 17th century still standing (look for the *anno domini* on the facade). The left side of the street is taken up by old warehouses that were once used for storage of exotic imported goods, but now serve as government offices. When you cross the little bridge in Strandgade and walk around the block to the right, you will come to a boatbuilding shop on the canal. Until the 1930s the shipyard of Burmeister and Wain was located on this square, but they ran out of space and moved farther out on Amager. Only small-scale industries have remained. The yellow house on the other side of the canal is **Søkvæsthuset**, with a library and a museum of naval history.

Cross the bridge again, turn left and then right at Wildersgade. **Café Wilder** and **Café Luna** on the corner of Sankt Annæ Gade are two of the places that give the neighbourhood its special charm: At

Vor Frelsers Kirke spire

lunchtime, lawyers from the ministries based here share the cafés with people from the free community of Christiania. Everybody is welcome in Christianshavn.

Further up Sankt Annæ Gade is **Vor Frelsers Kirke** (Our Saviour's Church) with its twirled spire. There are about 400 steps to the top, and you should try to climb them, if just to see the inside of the tower. The wooden construction is quite impressive, and halfway up you'll pass behind the huge clockworks.

Around the corner in Prinsessegade, there used to be military barracks. But in 1971 a group of hippies jumped the fence around the abandoned buildings and proclaimed the area a free community. Thus **Christiania** came into being, built on ideals of love, peace and brotherhood. In spite of police raids and several attempts from the government to normalise and legalise this social experiment, Christiania still survives. You are welcome to look around and maybe grab a bite to eat at **Spiseloppen** or have a drink at **Månefiskeren** (the Moon Fisher). Christiania doesn't have running water, central heating and the like. But the Christianites demand the freedom to live the way they like, build their houses according to their own needs and aesthetics, and also to smoke whatever they like, including pot. Hard drugs have been banned by the residents, but there is a busy market for marijuana in **Pusher Street**. The police do not look kindly on this traffic, so you should avoid taking pictures. Get your camera out again when you reach the lake, where some of the residents have built their own homes with great imagination and craftsmanship.

Turn left when you exit Christiania the way you came in, then left again on

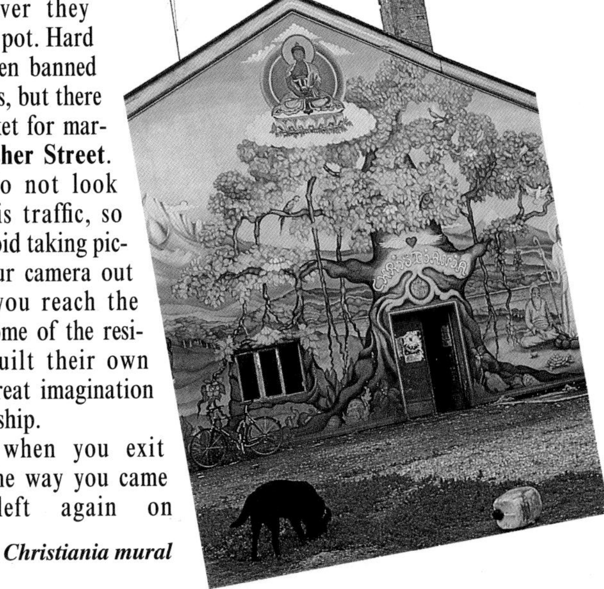

Christiania mural

Bådsmandsstræde and right on the old Christianshavns Voldgade. Follow this street across Torvegade and back to the canal. When the weather is good, you can rent a boat on the corner of Torvegade and paddle around in the harbour and the canal (summer only, 45kr. per hour). You can also do as the residents do and sit on the old wooden railings and enjoy a beer or a pastry from the bakery at **Christianshavns Torv**. This could be the place for your lunch break.

At home in Christiania

From this square, any of the buses will take you back across Knippelsbro to Slotsholmen. Get off at the first stop. **Holmens Kirke** to your right is the church of seafarers and of the navy. Inside is a curious reminder of how the traders became rich enough to build their warehouses on Christianshavn: the font is decorated with figurines of Moors and is tall enough to be used for the christening of negro slaves. Two Danish admirals, Tordenskjold and Jens Juel, have been buried in sarcophagi in the side chapel.

Holmens Kirke is situated next to **Slotsholmen**, which has been the seat of the government since the days of Absalon. The castle dominating the square is the fifth on these grounds; the first four were either consumed by fires or simply torn down. To experience the grandeur of the palace, find the door in the middle of the facade and walk through the building to the inner court. In the right wing, the Queen receives her guests on formal occasions, but when she does not occupy the reception rooms, the public can share in the splendour normally reserved for the privileged (tours in English start at 11am, 1pm and 3pm Tuesday–Sunday, May–September; October–December and February–April: tours at 11am and 3pm Tuesday, Thursday and Sunday; adults 25kr., children 10kr.). The left wing houses the parliament, the **Folketinget**. Debates are open to the public, but otherwise visitors are not welcome.

Continue into the grounds where the building to the left contains the royal stables and a carriage museum (Friday–Sunday 2-4pm; adults 10kr., children 5kr.). The old court theatre in the same building has been preserved since 1767, and now serves as a unique museum of theatre history (Wednesday 2-4pm, Sunday noon–4pm). To the left, there is a passage to the entrance of the Folketinget, and across from it another passage to **The National Library**. The pond in the middle of the library garden is what remains of a basin that Christian IV dug out for his warships. A few of the old mooring rings are in the wall behind the statue of Søren Kierkegaard.

From the Folketinget, turn down Tøjhusgade. Continue over Frederiksholm Canal to H.C. Andersens Boulevard and Copenhagen's finest art museum **Ny Carlsberg Glyptotek** (May–August: Tuesday–Sunday 10am–4pm, September–April noon–3pm; adults 15kr., children free; no charge Wednesday and Sunday). If the name rings a bell, it is no coincidence. The Carlsberg Breweries have always supported the arts, and the Glyptotek owns a world class collection of Egyptian, Greek, Roman and Etruscan sculpture along with paintings and sculpture by Degas, Gauguin, Rodin, van Gogh and many other not so famous artists. The rooms are centred around a peaceful winter garden.

The Glyptotek stands next to one of the entrances to the world-famous **Tivoli Gardens** (May–mid-September: 10am–midnight; adults 33kr., children 17kr.). Celebrating its 150th anniversary in 1993, Tivoli maintains its old-world charm, but has also changed with the times. Each season brings new additions to its offerings. Children come to ride the carousels, retired people just to sit and watch the flowers and the families. Pick up a free plan of the gardens at the main entrance.

For dinner, eating in Tivoli can be a bland and expensive experience, but there are exceptions. My own favourite is **Færgekroen** on the lake (Tel: 33 12 94 12, reservations necessary). The fare is standard Danish food with smørrebrød and some hot dishes. There is a free playground nearby, where parents are welcome to park their children. **Belle Terrasse** on the other side of the lake belongs in the upscale category (Tel: 33 12 11 36, reservations necessary). Another popular restaurant is **Grøften** behind the pantomime theatre (Tel: 33 12 11 25, reservations necessary). Do as the Danes do and order fresh shrimps on white bread and large mugs of beer.

At dusk, when lights and lanterns add a touch of magic to the fountains and flower beds, Tivoli changes character. Then the adults by far outnumber the children. At midnight it's all over, but on Wednesday, Friday and Saturday, Tivoli says good-night in style with a fireworks display at 11.45pm.

Night-time at the Tivoli Gardens

3. Frederiksberg

Behind the scenes at the Royal Copenhagen porcelain factory and Carlsberg Breweries, with sidetrips to the romantic Frederiksberg Have and the Zoo.

Blue-fluted porcelain

–Bus No 1 or 14 will take you from Rådhuspladsen to Royal Copenhagen at Smallegade 45. Get off at Søndre Fasanvej, cross the road and walk 100m (330ft) back the way you came.–

Every single piece of **Royal Copenhagen** porcelain is painted by hand. At the factory, you'll get to see how. The transformation of a simple white plate into a piece of art at the hands of one of their experienced painters is a fascinating process. No less interesting are the prices in the gift shop. Everything is second assortment and 30-50 per cent off, but the flaws are hard to find. The tour of the factory is free and lasts about an hour (tours start at 9, 10 and 11am).

Once you've done your tour, walk from the factory towards the city, but make a right turn at Andebakkestien (just before the first traffic lights) to get to the lovely **Frederiksberg Have**. Follow the lake to the left, then cross over the bridge and turn left. A Chinese pavilion, added in the romantic period of the early 19th century, sits on an island by itself. When you get to the fountain and Frederiksberg Castle stands in front of you, turn left and make your way out to the main gate, turning left and then right at the first fork in the path.

Across from the park lies the octagonal Frederiksberg Kirke. Despite its small size, the church has managed to attract some of the city's most popular priests, and consequently, it is much used for fashionable weddings.

Along Pile Allé, between the park and Vesterbrogade, you'll find a number of outdoor restaurants known as 'family gardens'. They serve traditional Danish *smørrebrød*, which should be savoured with beer and aquavit. But before lunch, you can also catch a glimpse of how the beer is produced at **Carlsberg Breweries** (tours are free and start at 11am and 2pm). Just continue uphill, stop where the road bends and turn left towards the elephant gate. You'll get to see the impres-

Chinese pavilion, Frederiksberg Have

sive old copper kettles for the malt and the just as impressive modern bottling hall with a capacity of 78,000 bottles per hour. The tour lasts about an hour, and, yes, they serve samples.

Carlsberg's elephant gate

Thus uplifted, make your way back to one of the family gardens or go down Valby Langgade to **Bjælkehuset** in No 2. The restaurants all serve the same kind of food, just trust your instinct on which one to choose. No matter which one you prefer, the **Copenhagen Zoo** will be nearby (Roskildevej 32, 9am–6pm in the summer, 9am–4pm in the winter; adults 45 kr., children 22 kr.).

The zoo has an acclaimed children's enclosure, where the young ones are allowed to pet the goats. Throughout the garden, they have the opportunity to also measure their own abilities against those of the (very docile) animals. Pick up directions in the information office.

Buses 6, 27 or 28 will take you back into town. If you have time, stop briefly at the **City Museum** near Vesterbros Torv (Vesterbrogade 59). From May through September, a ceramic model (which is pictured below) on the front lawn here shows Copenhagen as it looked in the 16th century – a mere village compared to the capital of today.

16th-century Copenhagen at the City Museum

4. Lyngby

Hiking, biking or sailing in the park areas around Lyngby.

–Take the S-train towards Hillerød, get off at Lyngby station and exit towards Jernbanepladsen. Alternatively, rent a bike in central Copenhagen (see Practical Information); remember to buy a separate train ticket for the bike. Boating (May–September): if you would like to rent a canoe, call 42 85 67 70 to reserve one in advance. You can also take a tour boat around the lakes. Call 45 87 01 52 for schedules (reservations not accepted). Bring swimsuits.–

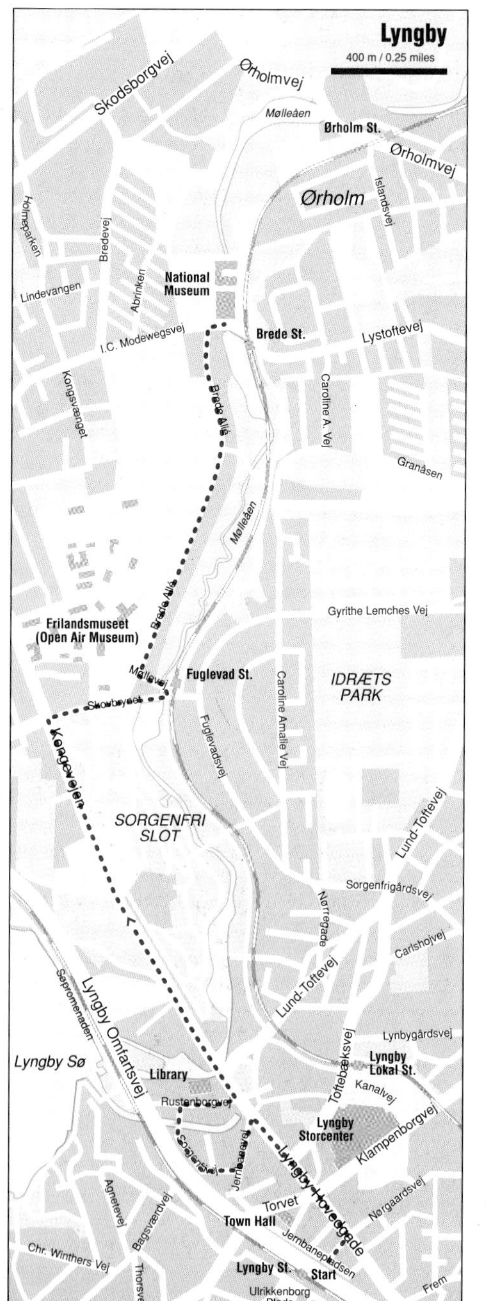

It takes just 20 minutes to get to Lyngby by train, but you'll feel like you are much farther away from the hustle and bustle of the city.

At Furesødal, you can rent a canoe for 50kr. per hour, or 250kr. for a full day. Bus 191 from Jernbanepladsen will take you there (get off where Nybrovej turns into Frederiksdalsvej). You'll have access to a couple of lakes and a brook, **Mølleåen**, which runs through **Dyrehaven** (the Deer Park).

If you don't want to do all the hard work yourself, boat-operators **Baadfarten** can take you around on the lakes instead. Proceed from the station down Jernbanevej, then make a left at Bagsværdvej and continue down Sorgenfrivej, where you'll find them at the bridge. For 50kr., you can buy an all-day ticket and sail across Lyngby and Bagsværd Lakes. Stop for an art exhibit at Sophienholm, or go for a walk in the woods – if you stay close to the lake, you can't possibly lose your way.

If you prefer to hike or bike,

Canoeing on the Mølleåen

follow Jernbanevej to Lyngby Hovedgade and turn left, pass the church and enter the park a little further up to your right. You'll be headed north, and if you exit in the north-west corner, **Frilandsmuseet** (the Open Air Museum) is just 200m (650ft) up the road (Kongevejen 100; open Easter–September: Tuesday–Sunday 10am–5pm; adults 20kr., children free). 40 old farmhouses from around the country have been transplanted onto the grounds of this museum. The houses are still furnished, and although you're not supposed to touch anything, you can still get to feel what life was really like in the old days in Denmark.

When you leave, go back down Kongevejen, turn left at Skovbrynet and left again at Møllevej after the lake. Møllevej turns into Brede Allé, which will take you to the village of **Brede**, once an important centre for production of copperware, but nowadays known as the home of a department of the **National Museum** as well as for **Brede Gamle Spisehus**, a very good, moderately priced restaurant (Tel: 42 85 54 57; Tuesday–Sunday noon–3pm and 5.30–9.30pm). The National Museum features two permanent exhibits: one is about the history of Mølleåen, the other about clothing and body culture (Tuesday–Friday; call 42 85 34 75 for prices and opening hours).

If you are tired of walking, catch the train back to Jægersborg S-train station. You can also walk on to the next stop in Ørholm. Bikes are not allowed on this particular train, so tired bikers will simply have to turn around, or ride the 7km (4¼ mile) to Klampenborg Station – left on Modewegsvej, then immediately right into the woods again, across Ørholmvej, left when you cross the railroad tracks, then right (follow the signs towards Strandmøllen and Klampenborg) and right again at Krudtmøllestien; when you get to the paved road in Raadvad, turn

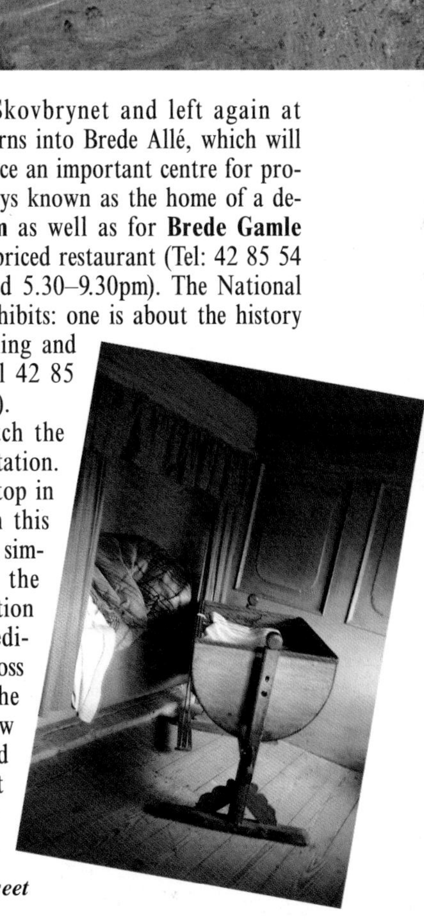

Farmhouse furnishings, Frilandmuseet

A pastoral scene, Mølleåen

left and go through the village, then turn left up Chauseen and stay on that trail the rest of the way. You'll get a good view of the ocean, and you should also be able to see some of the long-legged creatures that have given the Deer Park its name. The roads are somewhat hilly, so you'll deserve a drink at **Peter Lieps Hus** or in the amusement park **Bakken**, once you've finished this 12km (7 mile) tour.

Afternoon Itineraries

5. The Old Ramparts

A stroll through the parks of Copenhagen with side trips to nearby art museums.

–Take the S-train, or buses 5, 7, 14 or 16 to Nørreport Station.–

Copenhagen is praised as a green city – thanks to Christian IV. His many wars with the Swedes and the Germans forced him to think about its defence, and as a precaution, he planned a ring of ramparts and moats all the way around it. Although the circle has been broken in some places, you can still follow most of it through Tivoli, Ørstedsparken, Botanisk Have and Øster Anlæg to the Citadel in the north, and even across the harbour to Christiania.

The Botanical Garden

Start at the **Botanical Garden**, where every tree or shrub has a little name-tag attached. I rarely study them, but I like the garden for its variety and the beautiful greenhouse full of tropical plants (daily 10am–3pm; no charge). At the end of the garden, cross the road to get to the next park, **Østre Anlæg**. You'll still be following

In the Kunstindustrimuseet

the old moat: the large red building to the right is **The State Museum of Art** with collections of Danish artists and modern painters such as Picasso and Braque (Sølvgade 48; Tuesday–Sunday 10am–4.30pm; adults 20–40kr., children free). The smaller classical building to the left is **Hirschsprung's Collection** which specialises in Danish paintings from the golden age of the 19th century (Wednesday–Saturday 1–4pm, Sunday 11am–4pm; adults 20kr., children free).

When you exit Østre Anlæg, turn right and cross the railway tracks, then head for **Nyboder**, the low yellow buildings in front. These are the some of the quarters that Christian IV built for his marine soldiers, and even today they are rented exclusively to naval officers. Other military quarters are found at the **Citadel** in the park on the other side of Grønningen. Christian IV had left his line of ramparts unfinished when it reached the water, but his son Frederik III finished the work for him by creating the Citadel with five bastions and a double moat. Follow the moat to the entrance and walk straight towards the central square. The area is still a military reservation, so access is restricted. There is, however, one place where everybody can come, namely the library to the left of the church (on the 1st floor through the building and the garden).

If you scale the bastion behind the church, you'll see a Dutch windmill, where all the corn for the military bakery used to be

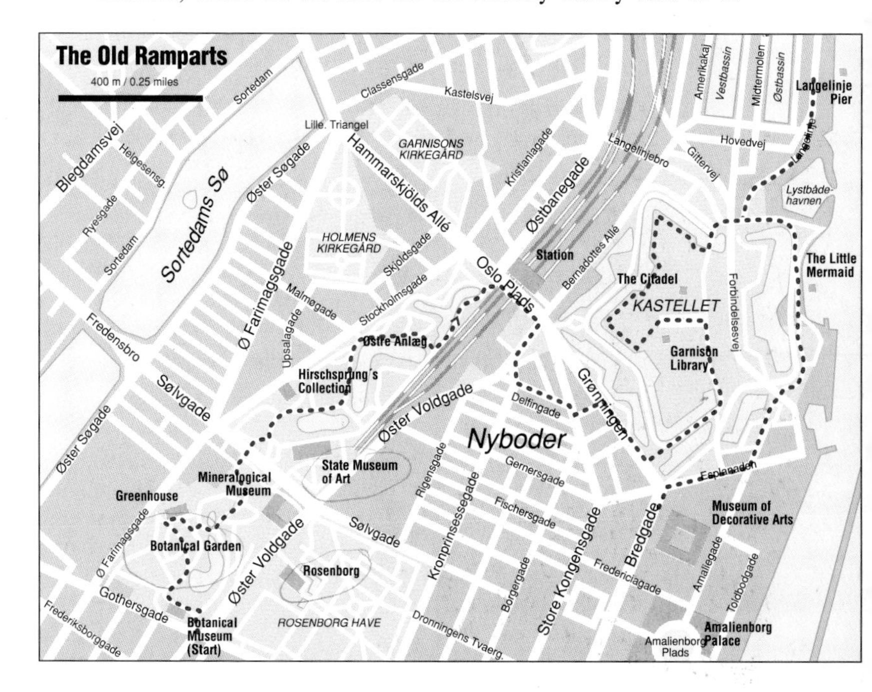

The Little Mermaid

ground. The mill is still tested once a year, on the Citadel's anniversary the 28th of October. Follow the path to the last bastion and exit towards the north. A staircase leads up to the road. turn right and walk towards the marina between **Langelinje Pier** and the *Little Mermaid.* Hans Christian Andersen's touching story about the mermaid who fell in love with a human prince and gave her voice in exchange for a pair of legs, only to see her loved one marry someone else, inspired the artist Edvard Eriksen. The statue is the trade mark for the Danish tourist organizations.

To get back to the city, you can catch the yellow HT sightseeing bus from the restaurant down the street or walk along the waterfront to Nyhavn. Consider a detour to **Kunstindustrimuseet** (the Museum of Decorative Arts) in Bredgade 68 with both medieval and modern design works (Tuesday–Sunday 1-4pm; adults 20-30kr., children free). Built around a garden, the museum makes an appropriate last stop on a tour of the parks.

6. Hellerup

For the whole family: the Experimentarium, Denmark's Aquarium, a trip to the beach and to the Bakken amusement park.

The Experimentarium, where science is fun

–Take bus 6 from Rådhuspladsen or Kongens Nytorv to Tuborgvej in Hellerup. The Experimentarium is located in the buildings of Tuborg Breweries to the right. Bring swimsuits for the afternoon.–

Did you hate physics in school? Then the **Experimentarium** will show you a couple of really neat things the teacher forgot to tell you about (Monday,

On Bellevue Beach

Wednesday and Friday 9am–6pm, Tuesday and Thursday 9am–9pm, Saturday and Sunday 11am–6pm; adults 50kr., children 35kr., one adult and one child: 70kr., 10 percent off). You can watch, touch and test some of the stranger phenomena of sound and light, dance in a discotheque where the music follows your movements, study your own skeleton and much more. It's hard to tell who gets more excited, kids or their parents.

Continue on bus 6 to **Charlottenlund Fort**. On the water side, you'll have a white sand beach, a large lawn and the ruins of a former military stronghold. To the other side lie the woods and Denmark's Aquarium, where you can study electric eels and other strange fish and shellfish (March–October: daily 10am–6pm, November–February: daily 10am–5pm; adults 30kr., children 15kr.; the fish get fed on Thursday and Sunday at 2pm). All in all, you can't find a better place to let the children loose with safety. There are also sufficient numbers of ice-cream vendors and hot dog stands plus a nice little circular café and sandwich bar.

Dyrehaven coachman

A similar piece of paradise lies 3.5km (2¼ miles) down the road. Get back on bus 6 to Klampenborg, where you'll have **Bellevue Beach** across from **Dyrehaven** (The Deer Park), and **Bakken** amusement park close by (just follow the signs). Bakken isn't quite as charming as Tivoli, but there is no entrance charge and four times as many amusements to try, ranging from water-slides to the traditional House of Horrors. For dinner, try Bakkens Perle (Tel: 31 64 31 64; 11am–midnight) or Peter Lieps Hus in Dyrehaven (Tel: 31 64 07 86; 9.30am–8pm).

7. Helsingør (Elsinore)

Kronborg Castle and the old merchants' houses, with side trips to the Science Museum, Louisiana Museum of Modern Art and even to Sweden.

–The Copenhagen Card will save you money on this trip. Make reservations for dinner (see below). Trains leave from the central railway station 25 and 55 minutes past the hour. When you exit Helsingør Station, you'll see Kronborg Castle in front of you, a 10-15 minute walk away.–

Helsingør is situated at the entrance to the narrow belt of water that separates Denmark from Sweden. For centuries, the city thrived because it could claim a 'sound due' from all ships passing through the belt. **Kronborg Castle** was erected around 1420 to ensure that the captains would pay their dues, with cannons pointing out over the water, and later modernised and expanded to the impressive Renaissance castle of today. Shakespeare found Kronborg an enticing backdrop for prince Amleth to ponder the essential questions of life and death, and the Danes also claim that Holger Danske, who is sitting asleep in the cellar, will come to their rescue if the nation is ever in dire need. Most of this castle is open, including the ball room, the church and the dungeon (May–September: daily 10.30am–5pm; April and October: Tuesday–Sunday 11am–4pm; November–March: Tuesday–Sunday 11am–3pm; adults 30kr., children 15kr.).

Kronborg Castle, inspiration for 'Hamlet'

If you are travelling with children, you should also consider a visit to **Teknisk Museum** (the Science Museum), with its displays of machines and inventions from the last three centuries. Take a taxi or bus 340 to Nordre Strandvej 23 (daily 10am–5pm; adults 24kr., children 12kr.).

If you need a coffee break when you get back to the harbour area, try the café in **Kulturhuset**, a former customs building that has been turned into a community centre. The tourist information office is here, from where you can get a free city map. The staff can also help you in case you'd like to stay overnight and maybe spend the next day on the beautiful Hornbæk Beach nearby.

Finding your way around Helsingør is not at all difficult. The

The famous ice-cream of Brostræde

city is laid out in a rectangle formed by [illegible] and Axeltorv [illegible] hours it is al- [illegible] et across the [illegible]. (with *Sund-* [illegible] it), and many [illegible] hopping across [illegible] ces are higher in [illegible] before you start [illegible] avian neighbours, [illegible] old Helsingør.

From Kulturhuset walk left towards the alley of Brostræde (famous for its ice-cream cones). Just two house numbers to the right, [illegible] narrower Gammel [illegible] can get an idea of what Helsingør looked like some [illegible]. Cross Stengade and continue up Sct. Annagade, where **Sankt Olai Church** will soon appear to your right (Monday–Friday 10am–2pm, May–August until 4pm). The church dates back to 1559, but the wall on the left of the entrance also carried the first church on the grounds, as far back as 1230. Notice the frescoes above the pulpit, typical of Danish churches from the Middle Ages. The christening chapel in the southwest corner is as old as the church, but the paintings of the apostles were added later.

When you come out, cross the street and follow Skt Olai Gade all the way to the end, then turn left. Between No 7 and 9, Munkegade starts. Follow it one block, then turn left, and you'll come to Stengade, the main pedestrian street. If you are not into shopping, just continue down Skyttenstræde to Strandgade. The oldest private house in Helsingør lies at No 27, half-timbered and erected in 1577. Strandgade will lead you back to the station.

Old Helsingør

About 8km (5 miles) south of Helsingør lies the **Louisiana Museum of Modern Art** (Gl. Strandvej 13, daily 10am-5pm; April–August: Wednesday, Saturday and Sunday until 10pm; adults 42 kr., children free). An outstanding collection of Henry Moore, Calder, Giacometti, Max Ernst etc, has made Louisiana the most visited art museum in the country. Even the architecture is an attraction, with a fine view of the water from the buildings, which are connected by a beautiful park. (Train to Humlebæk and follow the signs).

South of Louisiana lies the old hamlet of **Sletten**. Turn left when you leave Louisiana and follow Gammel Strandvej along the water. If you'd like to get back to Copenhagen, turn right on Oscar Brunsvej to get to the train station. But if you'd like to stay for dinner, follow all the twisting Gl. Strandvej until you get to **Sletten Kro** at No 137 (Tel: 42 19 13 01). It's somewhat pricey, but worth the money. You can also make a right turn, walk up to Strandvejen, catch bus 388 towards Lyngby and ride along the pretty coastline to Tårbæk, where you can dine at **Taarbæk Kro** (Tel: 31 63 00 96) with a nice view of the old marina. Bus 388 continues to Klampenborg Station (a 15–20 minute walk).

8. Roskilde

To the Church of the Kings, with side trips to the Viking Ship Museum, Ledreborg Palace and the Archaeological Research Centre in Lejre.

–The Copenhagen Card will save you money on this trip. Trains leave from the central railway station 03 and 33 minutes past the hour. In Roskilde, follow the signs towards 'Domkirken' or the tourist information.–

The **cathedral** or Church of the Kings rises majestically above the hills and the fjord of Roskilde, reminding visitors that this is a city

of importance. When Copenhagen was still a hamlet among many others, Roskilde was the capital of Denmark and one of the largest cities in Northern Europe. But ironically, the cathedral was founded at the same time as Absalon built his first castle in Copenhagen, and Roskilde has never regained the status it had.

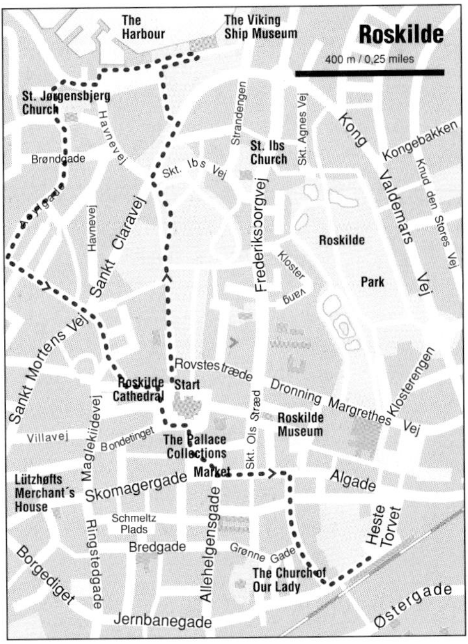

Since 1423, the cathedral has been the burial place for the kings and queens of Denmark. This tradition was initiated by Queen Margrethe I, whose body lies in a marble sarcophagus behind the altar. New side chapels have been added whenever space was needed. The latest addition is as recent as 1985, when Frederik IX was laid to rest behind the church. The cathedral is open to the public most of the time (call 42 35 27 00 to inquire about opening hours; adults 3kr., children 1kr.).

If you didn't see the Viking exhibit at the National Museum, you should consider a trip to the **Viking Ship Museum** at Roskilde Fjord (April–October: daily 9am–5pm, November–March: daily 10am–4pm; adults 28kr., children 18kr.). To get there, walk down through the park behind the cathedral to Sankt Claravej. On the way, you'll pass Sankt Hans Spring, where you can get a refreshing drink of cool water. The museum contains five ships that were recovered from the bottom of the fjord in 1962 plus a modern, full-size model and information on the technology of the Vikings. But don't get too excited: all that remains of the actual ships are some charred beams.

Roskilde is full of students

Proceed from the museum to the harbour and turn left up the stairs to **Sankt Jørgensbjerg**, the old part of town. Follow Kirkegade, Asylgade and Sankt Hansgade back to the cathedral. If you pass behind the church down Domkirkestræde and Sankt Ols Stræde, you'll come to Rosenhavestræde and the pleasant **Café Satchmo**.

Once you've seen enough of Roskilde, walk back to the station in

Roskilde Cathedral

time to catch the train leaving for Holbæk 30 minutes past the hour. The first stop is Lejre Station, where bus 233 will be waiting to take you to the **Historical-Archaeological Research Centre** (May–mid-October: daily 10am–5pm; adults 40kr., children 20kr.), situated here because Lejre was a central town in the early history of Denmark. You shouldn't be put off by the centre's name: its approach to the study of history is practical: every summer, selected families stay here for a week and try to live life as they did in the Iron Age or in the 19th century. As a visitor, you can follow them around, or even try to grind your own corn, or sail in a hollowed oak at the activity centre.

This part of the tour will be a hit with children, but at the next stop at **Ledreborg Palace** they must respect the usual 'do not touch' commands. It is easy to walk the 2km (1 mile) back to Ledreborg (June–August: daily 11am–5pm; access to the park all year; adults 40kr., children 10kr.), or you can wait for the bus which leaves 10 minutes before the hour.

At the research centre you got a glimpse of ordinary people's lives; Ledreborg will show you the much more elegant lifestyle of the aristocracy. Built by Count Johan Ludvig von Holstein around 1750, the palace still belongs to the Holstein family. The strict symmetry of the Versailles-style park and buildings is impressive, especially when viewed from the first floor, and the rooms are furnished from the late 18th century. In the basement is the dungeon and the old kitchen, which was still being used as late as 1950.

If you don't want to wait for the bus, you can walk back to Lejre railway station through the park (ask for directions).

Simulating the Iron Age at the Research Centre

Itineraries in Jutland

9. Århus

Through the Old Town museum and the actual old town of Århus, with stops at medieval churches and modern cafés.

–Pick up This Week in Århus, Ugen Ud *and a city map at the tourist information office in the town hall building; the staff can also tell you about tourist tickets for the buses. The Old Town is paved with cobblestones, so leave your high-heeled shoes at the hotel. Bus 3 towards Hasle runs from the town hall to the Old Town. Arrive before 10am to beat the crowds.–*

It seems like every kiosk in Denmark sells stacks of pretty postcards with pictures of quaint village idylls. The **Old Town** (Den Gamle By) is just such an idyll (Tel: 86 12 31 88, Viborgvej at Silkeborgvej; June, July, August: daily 9am–6pm, May and September: daily 10am–5pm, April and October: 10am–4pm, January–March and November: 11am–3pm, December: 10am–3pm; adults

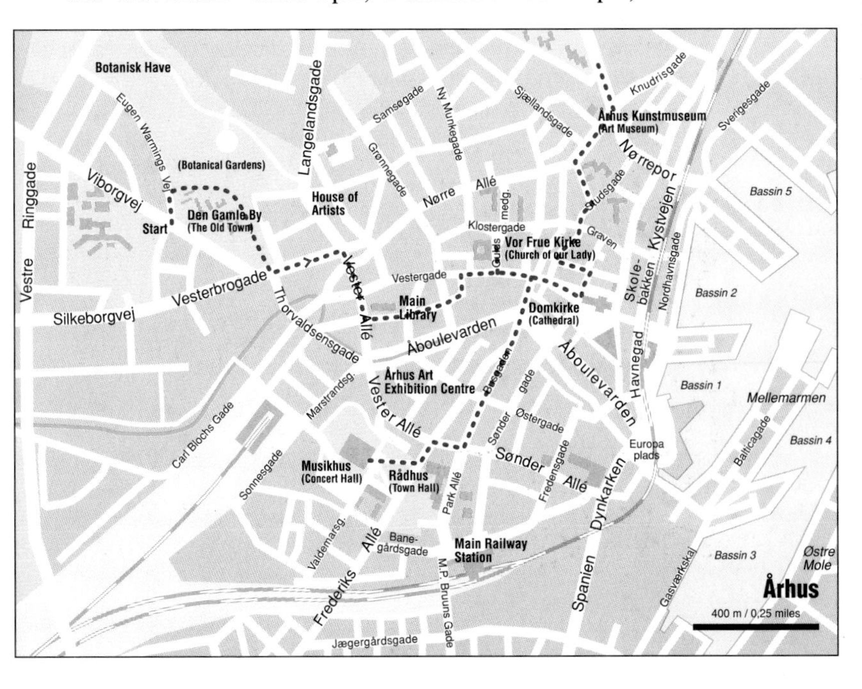

The Old Town of Århus

30/35kr., children 12kr.; you'll need a 20kr. brochure with a map). The only difference is that this is not a town but a museum, assembled of houses from all around the country. The school came from Funen, the post office from North Jutland, the pharmacy from South Jutland, and so forth. None of the buildings are inhabited, but they are all open, so you can see how they used to be furnished.

Each house represents a different trade: the hatter, the potter, the printer, the brewer, the tailor, the baker. At the bakery, you can even buy fresh sugar-sprinkled pringles and other goodies. If you would like a cup of coffee with them, there is also a nice cafeteria, **Simonsens Have**, where you are allowed to bring your own food if you don't want to buy theirs. There are classical concerts in the yard on summer Sundays.

When you exit, walk back towards the city alongside the town museum through the Botanical Garden. Turn left at Vesterbrogade. You can get proof that the old Århus is still alive if you look into the courtyard of No 32, where the well-known architects Friis and Moltke reside, but the surroundings are virtually untouched by their modern style. Turn right at Vesterbros Torv, then left when you reach the park area. The large building to your left is the public library (they have foreign newspapers in the reading room next to the cloak room). Continue down the narrow Møllestien and turn left where it ends, then right on Vestergade to get to **Vor Frue Kirke** (Church of Our Lady; Monday–Friday 10am–2pm, Saturday 10am–noon). The church once belonged to a monastery, and the old buildings are still standing. Like so many other monasteries, it survived the Reformation only because of its usefulness as a hospital for the poor. The complex dates back to around 1250, but during a renovation in the mid-1950s an even older church was discovered below the present one. This crypt church was reconsecrated and is now back in use again.

Just 300m (980ft) down the

Bakery, the Old Town

A cheerful visitor

street, the **cathedral** presides over Store Torv. Built in the early 13th century by bricklayers trained in southern Europe, it is the largest in the country. For a Lutheran church, it is richly decorated: the frescoes in the ceiling are outstanding, as are the Renaissance pulpit, the Dutch font, and the many memorial tablets on the walls.

The area behind the cathedral is so full of cafés that choosing one is difficult. They all serve good food, most of them at low prices. Try the streets around Volden, Graven, Klostergade and Studsgade. My own favourites are **Casablanca** in Rosensgade and **Englen** in Studsgade which has a charming patio in the back. After you've had your lunch, keep browsing. The cafés share the neighbourhood with lots of little shops – no hardware stores or auto part dealers, just lots of clothes, records, art and antiques.

An option for the afternoon is **Århus Kunstmuseum** (the Art Museum, Tuesday–Sunday 10am–5pm; adults 30kr., children free), which has a good collection of Danish paintings from the last two centuries and is equally quick to pick up on emerging trends in the art world. Turn right on Nørre Allé, then left on Nørregade. The museum lies in the south corner of Århus University campus, which is one of the nicest of its kind in the country – visitors are welcome to look around.

Walk back to the cathedral and up the pedestrian streets, or catch a bus (No 1, 11 or 14) back to the town hall. On the other side of the town hall square you'll find the **Music Hall** (Musikhus), a modern glass house with three large concert halls. There is a nice café in the foyer and a restaurant upstairs, and then of course, there is music. The Hall is open every night, so ask for a schedule at the ticket office. It is also the home of the National Danish Opera, which has made marathon Wagner performances a summer tradition. Another recurring event here is Århus Festuge, a festival that brings the whole city to its feet in September.

In the Café Casablanca

The nightlife and the restaurants in Århus are centred around the café district, Skolegade, and Vestergade behind the cathedral. A few bars are centred around Jægergårdsgade behind the train station. Look for inspiration in the *Nightlife* chapter.

Excursions from Århus

10. Silkeborg

To the beautiful lake country around Silkeborg, to the east of Århus, plus visits to the art museum and the Tollund Man. By paddle-steamer to Sky Mountain.

–Take the train from Århus to Silkeborg. If you like, you can easily reverse the itinerary by starting in Ry. If you are travelling with children, who might not enjoy 2½ hours on a boat, there is also a one-hour cruise on the lakes from Silkeborg.–

Silkeborg lies in one of the areas where the Danes go to spend their summer vacations. The country between Silkeborg and Skanderborg is as beautiful as can be. Criss-crossed by quiet rivers, it provides the ideal setting for canoeing or hiking trips, or just for lazy days spent in the sun with a picnic basket. A couple of first-class museums in Silkeborg finish the picture off.

When you get to Silkeborg train station, exit at Drewsensvej and walk down Estrupsgade to Skoletorvet, where you'll find **Galerie Moderne** in No 39. Don't be fooled by the surroundings – it is one of the best galleries in Denmark, specialising in modern, abstract art by people such as Corneille and Alechinsky plus some of the top names in Denmark: *Asger Jorn*, *Peter Brandes* and many others. If you like what you see, there is more at the **Silkeborg Art Museum**. Walk back towards the station and turn left on Drewsensvej; when it turns into a path, follow it for one more block, then turn right at Åhavevej and continue past the canoe rental shops to Åhave Allé. The museum stands on top of the hill (use the stairs next to the ice cream parlour). To catch up with the rest of the itinerary, just stay on Åhavevej when you walk back.

If abstract art is not your cup of tea, ignore the Galerie Moderne and take the first right from Skoletorvet and walk all

Tollund Man

the way down Nygade; **Café Picasso** on the intersecting Tværgade is a nice place to stop for something to drink or a freshly-made sandwich. Turn left on Søndergade, which will take you to the town hall square; turn right and walk down the passage on the right side of the church. The **Silkeborg Museum** of local history (Tel: 86 82 14 99; daily 10am–5pm during the summer; adults: 20kr., children: 5kr.) lies on the other side of Christian VIII's Vej. Here again, Silkeborg has a first-rate sight hidden behind a local label: the **Tollund Man** is the remarkably well-preserved body of a man who died about 2,200 years ago. A rope around his neck shows that he was hanged before he was thrown into a bog. The acidic peat served as a natural defence against decay. When he was found, a young boy had been reported missing, and the police were called in to check the body. However, the peat above him was compact and had not been touched for centuries. His face is so lifelike that you can see even the stubbles on his chin. He looks relaxed and at ease, as if he is just sleeping.

The museum lies close to the water, from where you can rent a canoe or take a tour boat out on Julsø Lake. The most famous of the boats is *Hjejlen* (The Plover), which has been sailing on the lake since 1861. It is the oldest paddle wheeler still in use in the world, and it will take you on an unforgettable cruise to **Himmelbjerget**. *Hjejlen* sails only twice a day (10am and 1.45pm, late June–mid-August), and you have to be there at least half an hour in advance, since they don't take reservations (there are other boats than *Hjejlen* which don't fill up as quickly). The trip takes 1 hour and 15 minutes each way and allows you one hour on Himmelbjerget; you can have lunch on board.

Tower of Himmelbjerget

Himmelbjerget translates as the Sky Mountain. A slight exaggeration, perhaps, because although this is one of the highest peaks in the country, it reaches just 147m (482ft) above sea level. But look at it this way: scaling a hill this size is not difficult, and the view from the top is just as magnificent.

There is a beautiful 7km (4¼ mile) trail to the small town of Ry through the woods. If you don't want to go back the way you came, you can also take the boat back to Ry and the train to Århus from there. But maybe you noticed the good restaurants in Silkeborg's Nygade. **Café Piaf** at No 31 offers good, French food at moderate prices, and **Den Go'e Fe** (the Good Fairy) at No 18 has many vegetarian dishes on the menu. Afterwards, sit outside at **Musikværkstedet** (No 18, in the backyard) and listen to jazz or folk music.

The 'Hjejlen' has been sailing since 1861

11. Djursland

Along country roads north of Århus to manor houses, Stone Age monuments and old farming and fishing villages.

–This excursion is planned for those who are driving, but you can also get to most of the places by bus – the last paragraph will tell you how. –

The beautiful peninsula of Djursland lies just half an hour's drive north of Århus. If you look at a map of Denmark, Jutland (the mainland) looks like a man with a pointed hat, his one eyebrow being Mariager Fjord, his mouth Horsens Fjord and Djursland his dripping nose. The drips are Mols Bjerge, a beautiful hill country that got its present shape when the ice receded some 15,000 years ago.

Pretty as it is, Djursland has always been a popular place. You turn a corner, and a 4,000-year-old gravemound appears out in a field. Just a few kilometres further away it might be a Renaissance manor house that greets you. And on the way from one sight to the next you will pass through charming little villages with 13th-century Romanesque churches and 17th-century farmhouses.

Driving up from Århus, stay off the freeway and follow the Daisy-route from Skæring (a Daisy-map is available at most fuel stations and bookstores for 35kr.). As soon as you have passed through Hornslet, **Rosenholm Castle** will appear on your left (tours of the castle in English start 30 minutes past the hour 10.30am–4.30pm and last about an hour; adults 40kr., children 20kr.). Built in 1559, in part with bricks from nearby Kalø Castle, Rosenholm is one of the finest Renaissance castles in the country, complete with a moat, towers and a beautiful park with peacocks.

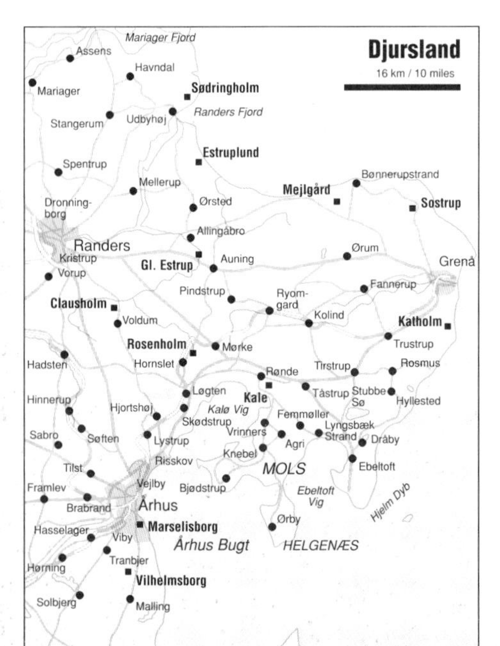

Stay on the Daisy-route. It continues through Mørke and Rønde to **Mols Bjerge**, where it will take you through the villages Vrinners, Agri, Knebel, and Vistoft – strange names, even to a Danish ear. Between Agri and Knebel, look for **Posekjær Stenhus**, a large round Stone Age cairn. The outer ring of rocks supposedly keeps evil spirits away. There were originally three graves in the middle; that's why the remaining one appears to be off-centre.

Some of the farms here sell their own produce from stalls along the road. Often each stall is nothing more than a shelf with an empty jar serving as the cash register. The prices are listed on a piece of cardboard, and you just help yourself to the cherries (*kirsebær*), berries (*bær*), apples (*æbler*), pears (*pærer*), peas (*ærter*), carrots (*gulerødder*) or whatever is in season and leave exact change.

Do not turn left inland, but stay on the road along the coast following the Daisy-route until you get into **Ebeltoft**. There are a couple of parking areas next to the post office on the waterside, and the pedestrian street is just one block away from the water. Ebeltoft is a lovely old town, but this is no secret, so on a good summer's day there will be thousands of people here. But it is easy to get away from the crowds: once you have gone through the centre, just stay on the south side of the central square. If you would like to know more about Ebeltoft, pick up the free tourist brochure in the old town hall. On Saturdays, this building is still used for weddings. For lunch in Ebeltoft, the restaurant **Mellem Jyder** at the beginning of Juulsbakke has the kind of old-fashioned provincial ambience that the cafés rebel against.

Posekjær Stenhus, a Stone Age cairn

Exit the old part of town through Toldbodgade (off Juulsbakke). The yellow house at the end of the street is a unique museum of modern glass works. Five hundred artists from different countries have submitted some of their best works, and the museum has such a large collection of glass sculpture that it has to change the exhibition frequently in order to do justice to all the artists. They have glass kites, glass portrait busts and other unusual items. (**Glasmuseet**, Strandvejen 8; mid-May–mid-September: daily 10am–5pm,

Rosenholm Castle

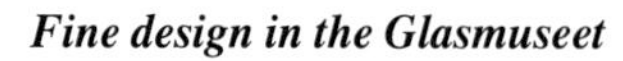

Fine design in the Glasmuseet

March–mid-May and mid-September–December: 1–4pm, closed January and February; adults 20kr., children 5kr.).

About 200m (650ft) to the right, *Fregatten Jylland* (*Frigate Jutland*) is undergoing extensive restoration. She was built in 1860 as the largest wooden ship of the navy and has cruised as far away as the West Indies. Although she was a good sailor and did well in a fight with the Prussians in 1864, she has long since been retired. The restoration will continue through 1994, but it is already possible to get on board and study her construction first hand (Strandvejen 4; daily 10am–5pm; adults 20kr., children 10kr.).

Leaving Ebeltoft to the north catch the Daisy-route again and turn right towards **Dråby**. The village church is worth stopping for because it is unusually large and spacious for a village church and is beautifully decorated with frescoes. **Hyllested Church** also has frescoes but of an earlier and much more frivolous kind: Adam and Eve are portrayed embarassedly clutching their fig leaves, but the painter didn't give the devil similar protection.

From Hyllested you can continue to Rosmus and turn left towards Tirstrup, where you'll hit the main road back to Århus. But if the day is still young and you would like to see some more, turn right a few kilometres after Tirstrup and follow the signs towards Kolind and Ryomgård. Stay on the road until you get to Auning (via Pindstrup), then turn left. On the other side of Auning you'll soon see the impressive structure of the **Gammel Estrup** manor house. The interiors are not quite as extravagant as those at Rosenholm, but still worth seeing. A new **Museum of Agriculture**, located in the farm buildings, adds an interesting contrast. It shows just how much hard work it took to survive in the country in the old days. You can see the tools used 200 years ago, and a contemporary farmer's kitchen is pitted against the kitchens of 100 and 200 years ago. The museum shows how hard-working farm labourers have been substituted by machines, both inside their buildings and outside.

To get back to Århus at the end of this long day, turn right in Auning and follow road 563. You'll get back on to the Daisy-route south of Hvilsager, this time traveling towards Århus.

By **Public Transport**: Catch bus 123 to Ebeltoft, leaving from the coach terminal in Århus at 20 minutes past the hour (Monday–Friday). When you have seen Ebeltoft, consider a trip through Mols Bjerge on a local bus. Route 1 will take you past the Posekjær Cairn. If you like, get off at the main stop in Knebel and stroll down to the water, until the bus comes back half an hour later. Alternatively, you can take No 119 from Århus to Rosenholm Castle at 8.40 or 10.40am and either continue to Gammel Estrup two hours later or go back to Løgten, where you can change to bus 123 to Ebeltoft. Call 86 12 86 22 to verify times.

NORTH JUTLAND

12. Skagen

The art museums of old Skagen followed by lunch on the wharf, then a visit to the open air museum in Skagen Vesterby, and finally to Grenen, the tip of Jutland. Finish on a fine beach.

–Skagen is on a peninsular about 2km (1¼ mile) long and Grenen another 2km away. If you rent a bicycle (see Practical Information) it is no distance, but if you walk, I recommend that you visit the museums and Grenen on one day and save Vesterby and the sand-buried church for the next. That will give you two half days to spend on the beach.–

Skagen's claim to fame is not just that it lies at the very tip of Jutland, where the land nose-dives into the sea. The town would be an attraction in itself, even if nature had been less intriguing. With its charming yellow houses and white picket fences, the town is just as picturesque as Ebeltoft or Helsingør. In addition, some of the best Danish painters of the late 19th century settled in Skagen, among them P.S. Krøyer and Michael and Anna Ancher, whose style is often labelled as Scandinavian impressionism. Some people come to Skagen just to visit the local art museum.

From the train station, walk up Sct Laurentii Vej (towards Grenen) until you see a sign for Brøndums Hotel on your right. **Skagen Museum** is located on this road, and the museum gives a good introduction to life on Skagen (Brøndumsvej, tel: 98 44 64 44; June–August: daily 10am–6pm, winter: 1pm–4pm except Monday; adults 25kr., children free). Whether it is a painting of Marie Krøyer and Anna Ancher walking on the beach at sunset or of fishermen dragging a boat onshore, these works portray situations that can still be seen, even if people doing such things today don't

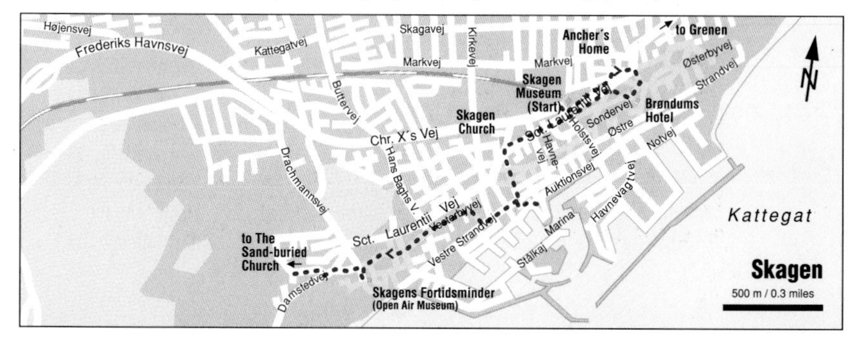

Picturesque Skagen, at the tip of Jutland

wear the same clothes as they do in the paintings.

The artists used to meet at **Brøndums Hotel**, and you should also treat yourself to a cup of coffee here while you watch people go by. Anna and Michael Ancher lived close by, and you can retrace their steps from the hotel through the neighbourhood to their house at Markvej 2. Walk around the hotel and follow Østerbygade, then take the first side street to the left. When you reach the end of the street, walk towards the water tower and you'll be there (Tel: 98 44 30 09; June–August: daily 10am–6pm, winter: 11am–3pm except Monday; adults 25kr., children 5kr.). The house was originally more sparsely furnished than it is now, but the style is the same. There are paintings everywhere, and even the door frames have been decorated with pretty flowers. Some sketches and unfinished paintings are exhibited next door at **Saxilds Gård**.

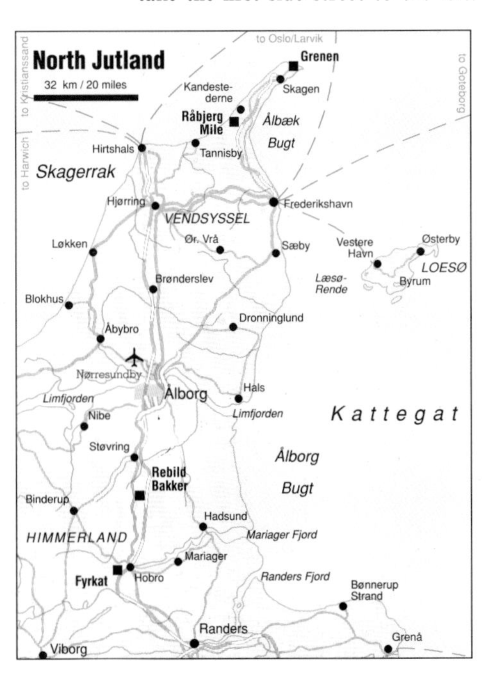

Follow Sct Laurentii Vej back, then turn right on Kappelgangen to get to **Skagen Church**. The church is newly renovated and provides a peaceful break from the busy streets. Just about every church near the coast has ship models hanging from the ceiling, as here. They were put up by fishermen who hoped that their sea trips would henceforth be blessed with calm weather and a safe return.

Fishing is still an important trade in Skagen, and most of the

Skagen's sand-buried church

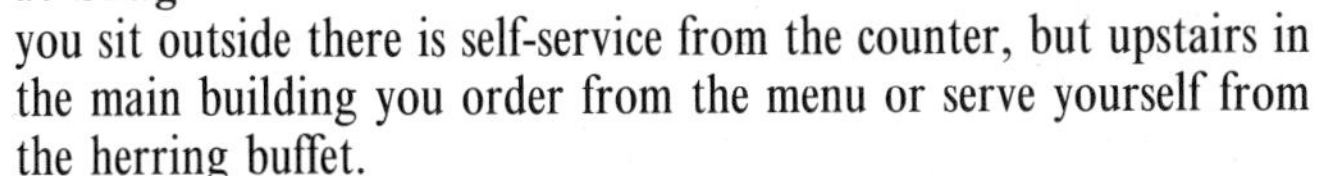

harbour area is reserved for storage or transportation companies. But there is a large marina in the centre which is where half the town gathers at lunchtime. To get there, walk across Sct Laurentii Vej and continue down Trondsvej. Most people buy a tray with fishcakes, smoked herring, fried calamari or some other fish-based dish from one of the little shops, but you can also sit down at **Skagen Fiskerestaurant.** If you sit outside there is self-service from the counter, but upstairs in the main building you order from the menu or serve yourself from the herring buffet.

When you leave the harbour, find Vesterbyvej (it runs parallel to Sct Laurentii Vej). This street turns into Svallerbakken, which ends at **Skagen Fortidsminder**, the open air museum of local history (P.K. Nielsensvej, tel: 98 44 47 60; May–September: daily 10am–5pm, March–April and October–November: Monday–Friday 10am–4pm; adults 20kr., children 2kr.). There's a striking contrast here between the house of a wealthy fisherman and that of his poor colleague, who lived with his parents, his wife and six children in just one room. The museum also shows how Skagen has changed over the years, from a village of black wooden buildings to the yellow and red brick houses of today. One of the halls is dedicated to the many men, both young and old, who never came back from sea.

About 1km (0.6 mile) further south, you'll find one of the eeriest reminders of Skagen's struggle with nature. Out in the middle of the woods, a lonesome church tower rises between the trees. When you get closer, it turns out that there is nothing left but the tower. The church was erected in the 14th century at a safe distance from the beach, but the sand kept moving closer, and by the late 18th century, the parishioners had to dig their way to church. In 1795, they finally gave up and tore down the main building, but they left the tower standing (June–September: 11am–5pm; adults 7kr., children 3kr.). The trees in the area have been planted to keep the sand from drifting any further. Walk down Gammel Kirkesti (across Damstedvej), then you'll see the forlorn tower in the distance.

Ocean wrestling at Grenen

Damstedvej leads down to a really nice beach, less crowded than its counterpart north of Skagen. But if you don't have your swimsuit with you, you should head all the way up north to

Grenen for a spectacular view of the ocean instead. At the tip of Jutland, Kattegat wrestles with the North Sea, and it looks like an even fight. You can stand with one foot in each ocean, but be careful, because the current is strong. (Swimming is not only prohibited here, but extremely dangerous.)

A bus leaves for Grenen from the train station, but it is also within walking distance (4km/2½ miles from the south end of Skagen, 2km from the north end). Just before you reach Grenen you can get a great view of the whole area from the top of the lighthouse. Grenen is always popular, but is never more so than around sunset, the local rush hour.

On Råbjerg Mile, a travelling dune

13. Kandestederne

Swimming in the west coast surf near Skagen, with lunch at the romantic Hjorths Hotel, then past a travelling sand dune to Gammel Skagen.

–Bring swimming gear. During the high season, bus 99 leaves from the railway station at irregular intervals (ask for a schedule at the train station). Get off in Kandestederne (a 25-minute ride).–

Skagerrak is a docile sea compared to its neighbour on the west coast. The beaches of Skagen town are pleasant, but you shouldn't leave North Jutland without a taste of the North Sea waves. **Kandestederne** is one of the best beaches to go to. Don't envision beach chairs and cocktail waitresses, because here you'll only find a flat white sand beach and the powerful west-coast surf. In Kandestederne nature provides free entertainment for those who like to ride the waves and get their faces wet. It is not the best place to bring small children, but a 5 or 6-year-old should be able to hold his own against the waves, and enjoy it too.

Kandestederne has another advantage: when you get tired of playing, you can put your clothes back on and walk a few hundred meters up to **Hjorths Hotel**, where they have a wonderful restaurant and a pizza bar in the back. It eases the transition from beach bum back to civilised human being.

If you are into hiking and still have the energy, ask a member of the staff at the hotel to point out the way to Råbjerg Mile. You can follow the paved road or walk off the road, which is a little harder but much more interesting. After about 5km (3 miles) you

Gammel Skagen, threatened by sand dunes

might think that you have walked all the way to the east coast and that the water waits right behind the dunes. It is not so. You have reached **Råbjerg Mile**, a travelling sand dune that took off from the west coast hundreds of years ago, and is still moving slowly towards the east. In another 150 years, it will block the only road to and from Skagen and force future generations to come up with a creative response to nature's challenges.

From Råbjerg Mile, follow the road. A couple of potters have set up shop along the last stretch of the road, and their prices are somewhat lower than in the city. Catch the bus back, but don't go all the way to Skagen, get off in **Gammel Skagen** on the west coast. (Or you could jump on the bus in Kandestederne and let it take you all the way to Gammel Skagen. Don't stop at Råbjerg Mile, the next bus might be hours away).

Gammel Skagen lies where the fishermen first settled, hoping that they could make a living out of fishing in the North Sea. They could, but they had not foreseen that the land would be just as treacherous as the sea. As at Råbjerg Mile, the sand kept creeping up around their houses, and fighting the sand became as much of a concern as fighting the North Sea storms. The town we now know as Skagen grew up because life at the original Skagen simply had become too hard.

But if you arrive on a sunny summer's afternoon, Gammel Skagen only looks inviting. It is not a big place – one paved main road and a dozen or two dirt roads. There are a couple of restaurants, largely overpriced, but if you don't want to spend the money for dinner, try to get by on snack foods until sunset. One of the roads in Gammel Skagen is named **Solnedgangen** (The Sunset), and that is where you should be when everybody comes out to watch the sun dip into the sea.

Sunset, Gammel Skagen

Denmark is known to be an expensive country, but that doesn't mean you can't find bargains. The tourist brochures will try to sell you fur coats and furniture and other such major investments, and they do a good job at that, so I'll concentrate on things that will fit in your suitcase and hopefully won't turn your wallet inside out.

A warm welcome for shoppers

Everything you purchase is subject to a 25 percent sales tax called *moms*. As a tourist you can get the *moms* on major purchases refunded at the border. Pick up a tax free brochure in one of the many shops that advertise tax free shopping.

Danish Design

Furniture, kitchenware, stereos, textiles, toys – anything that can be designed can also be labelled Danish design. The style is what counts. 'Form follows function' was the phrase that Scandinavian designers built their reputation on. The best place to study the results are in Illums Bolighus and Illum's, two of the shops on Strøget in Copenhagen. *Stelton* bottle openers and bar equipment, for example, or *Kirk* telephones.

Porcelain

Royal Copenhagen and Bing & Grøndahl are two famous labels in Danish porcelain. Today, they actually belong to the same company, but they still

Bang & Olufsen telephone

operate under both names. Visit the stores on Strøget in Copenhagen to study the many beautiful designs. But if you are not a collector and are just looking for a souvenir, buy a 'second' (slightly imperfect) or shop at one of the flea markets. You can recognise 'seconds' from the stamp on the bottom, which has been scratched a little by the factory.

Glass and ceramics

Within the last decade, a new generation of glass-blowers has appeared out of nowhere and breathed new life into a dying craft. Illums Bolighus in Copenhagen has a large collection of the new glasses, bowls and vases, but you can also find them in gift stores around the country. There is a glass-blower in Skagen next to the train station, and he has colleagues in Copenhagen in Christiania and Rosenborg Garden (Kronprinsessegade 34B). During the summer, glass-blowers take turns demonstrating their art at the Glass Museum in Ebeltoft. Traditional glassware can be purchased from Holmegaard (Østergade 17 in Copenhagen).

Similarly, there are a large number of potters at work these days. Their products are mainly sold in gift stores, but you can also buy directly from the artisans. Look out for signs when you are driving along country roads.

Flea market browser

Flea markets

If you are visiting during the summer, don't miss the flea markets in Copenhagen. There is one on Israels Plads (close to Nørreport train station) and another in Smallegade at Frederiksberg behind the town hall. Bus 14 runs by both of them. The dealers get most of their goods from estate sales, and you can always find blue-fluted Royal Copenhagen porcelain there, along with Christmas plates, crystal vases, Holmegård glassware and other good stuff, if you take your time to weed through the junk to find the gems.

Clothes

The pedestrian streets are filled with people who shop for clothes, so just follow them – or your nose. The department store *Magasin* (Bremerholm in Copenhagen, Immervad in Århus) always has a sale somewhere in the house. For discount items, try Daells Varehus (Nørregade 17 in Copenhagen) or Salling (Søndergade in Århus).

Danish Knitwear

Franco Sko also has several outlets in Copenhagen with shoes at discount prices (eg Købmagergade 43).

Leather

If a fashion fur from Birger Christensen is not in your budget, how about a leather coat from one of the discount stores on Vesterbrogade in Copenhagen? You can get a good jacket for about 1,000kr. (250kr. deductable for *moms*).

Knitwear

When the cold, rainy-grey winter comes around, woollen sweaters turn into friends. That's why knitwear has become almost an art form in the Scandinavian countries. You'll find traditional patterns at Kaufmann (Nygade 2) and Sweater Market (Frederiksberggade 15), both on Strøget in Copenhagen. If you would like a more modern style, walk around the corner to Nicole Garn (Vestergade 12), where you can also buy the wool and patterns to the models on display.

Jewellery

Amber still washes up on the coast from time to time, and you'll find amber stores in all the tourist areas. You can get a pair of earrings for 50kr. if you look around. Another Danish speciality is exact copies of Viking and Bronze Age jewellery (Grønnegade in Copenhagen; Kannikegade 12 in Århus). Halberstadt on Strøget in Copenhagen (Østergade 4) has its own tourist attraction: an 18kt. gold model train with wagons full of diamonds, rubies, emeralds and sapphires. Gerda Lyngaard nearby (Østergade 15) interprets amber and other materials in a dramatic new way. In the side streets off Strøget, you can find young jewellers who sell their own designs, for instance Guld & Gummi (Gammel Mønt 37) and Metal Point (Pilestræde 42). Erle Perle (Skindergade 33) doesn't care for silver and gold, but makes colourful earrings out of plastic, wood and other inexpensive materials.

Amber everywhere

Eiderdowns

Here's a secret that every Dane knows: to buy one of the fabulous Danish eiderdown comforters at half price, go to Jysk Sengetøjslager, a discount chain with outlets all around the country (in Copenhagen on Vesterbrogade 65 and Østerbrogade 116). Nobody can beat their prices. Remember to buy covers for your eiderdown, and ask the store to pack it tightly so you can travel with it (it won't do it any harm).

Food

Everything you've seen on the restaurant menus can also be found in the stores, but some things are easier to travel with than others. Although the speciality stores often have the highest quality, you will be better off if you shop in a supermarket, where the food is vacuum-packed. For instance, an ordinary, semi-strong Danish cheese has such a strong smell that it could ruin your suitcase if not properly wrapped. Guld Danbo or Klovborg are two of my favourites, not too strong but with a lot of taste. Then there is the black bread, the *leverpostej* (liver paté), the sweet-pickled cucumbers, the North Sea caviar, the smoked salmon, the biscuits, you name it... And don't miss the black liquorice. You'd have to be raised on the stuff to enjoy Piratos, but try Domino, Skiltelakrids and Saltbomber. If you prefer something sweet, Sømod (Nørregade 36 in Copenhagen) makes its own drops in all sizes and flavours.

Special Souvenirs

Toy theatres were popular in the old days. Hans Christian Andersen loved them, and you might too when you see the selection at Priors Dukketeatre. They have the Royal Theatre in miniature, as well as whole plays in packages or in single figures. It's easy to get lost in this enchanting little world. Unfortunately, their lease has been terminated, so I can't tell you where to find the new shop. Call them at 33 15 15 79 to get the latest address.

And don't leave the country without a package of candles. Even if you bring nothing else home with you, you should at least buy this inexpensive little creator of genuine Danish *hygge*.

Pick and mix

Every neighbourhood has its own cafés. Take advantage of them. Most cafés have a quiche on the menu, as well as one or two salads, *chili con carne*, different kinds of sandwiches and maybe a soup. You order and pay at the bar, and they'll bring the food to your table. It's simple, filling, inexpensive – and often delicious.

Danish beer, internationally famous

During a typical, normal day, a Dane will eat bread with cheese or jam for breakfast, and maybe a portion of yoghurt or muesli. On Sundays, he'll go to the bakery and buy bread and pastries: *rundstykker*, *kryddere*, *tebirkes* and *chokoladeboller* (try them!). For lunch he'll have *smørrebrød* or a salad. In the afternoon, he might sneak out to the hot-dog stand, or buy pastries (*wienerbrød*) or a bag of candy to get him through the rest of the day. But what he'll eat for dinner is hard to predict. It might be a pizza, a load of potatoes with gravy and traditional meatballs (*frikadeller*), a slice of lean meat with a salad on the side, or a spicy curry-dish.

Traditional food often includes things that have been smoked, salted or pickled, while the younger generations prefer their dishes to be fresh, crisp and/or spicy hot.

Copenhagen

Traditional Danish Food

CAFÉ SORGENFRI
Brolæggerstræde 8
Tel: 33 11 58 80
If you can cut your way through the smoke, you're in for a treat: Danish *smørrebrød* served in an old-fashioned bar that hasn't changed for decades.

CAFÉ CHARLOTTENBURG
Nyhavn 2
Tel: 33 13 11 58
You don't have to see the exhibit at Charlottenburg to enjoy the excellent *smørrebrød* in the café.

Smørrebrød with cheese

Hansens Gamle Familiehave
Pile Allé 10–12
Tel: 36 30 92 57
Romantic courtyard. You are allowed to bring your own food, as long as you buy something to drink, but their food is inexpensive and good.

Grøften
Tivoli
Tel: 33 12 11 25
VIPs and commoners eat and drink side by side in this old-fashioned Tivoli restaurant. Order shrimps on white bread, the house speciality.

Cafés

Although most cafés offer something to eat, the following have a larger selection of good food at affordable prices. They don't take reservations, just walk on in.

Scala
Vesterbrogade 2E across from Tivoli
Tel: 33 15 12 15
Scala looks like a shopping centre, as indeed it is, but it is full of inexpensive cafés too.

Sommersko
Kronprinsensgade 6
Tel: 33 11 08 41
Sommersko has about 40 items on the menu, all of them good and very reasonably priced. The portions are huge, so don't order more than one item at a time.

Café Emma
Østerbrogade 64
Tel: 35 26 09 52
A nice, old-fashioned café at Østerbro where the food is displayed behind glass, so you can point at what you want.

Hackenbusch
Vesterbrogade 124
31 21 74 74
Vesterbro's most popular café also serves some of the best inexpensive meals in town.

Kafé Rust
Guldbergsgade 8
Tel: 31 35 00 33
You can't get good food any cheaper. It's luxury for budget travellers.

Barcelona
Fælledvej 21
Tel: 31 35 76 11
Café downstairs, restaurant upstairs. The menu changes, but it's always good. Reservations recommended.

A tradition of good service

Delicious summer spread

Steak Houses

Peder Oxe
Gråbrødre Torv 11
Tel: 33 11 00 77
Serve yourself from the delicious salad bar while you wait for your steak to arrive.

Bryggeriet Apollo
Vesterbrogade 3
Tel: 33 12 33 13
Brews its own beer and orders its own meat, but still keeps prices at a moderate level.

Din's
Lille Kannikestræde 3
Tel: 33 93 87 87
Cook your own steak on a sizzling hot stone plate.

Jensens Bøfhus
Kultorvet 15
Tel: 33 15 09 84
Also at: Gråbrødre Torv
Tel: 33 32 78 00
If you have a craving for steak, but cringe when you look at most establishments' prices, this place will save you and your wallet.

Vegetarian

Zeze
Ny Østergade 20
Tel: 33 14 23 90
If you happen to be in the neighbourhood around lunch time, stop for a freshly mixed salad at this trendy little café.

Riz Raz
Kompagnistræde 20
Tel: 33 15 05 75
Serve yourself from a large buffet of salads and vegetable dishes prepared as in Mediterranean countries. You can also order meat on the side.

Shezan
Viktoriagade 22
Tel: 31 24 78 88
Half of Copenhagen knows and loves this family-run Indian restaurant on Vesterbro, with neon lights in the ceiling but good and plentiful meals for little money. They serve meat-dishes too.

Urtens Café
Larsbjørnsstræde 18
Tel: 33 15 03 52

PØLSEVOGN

Select your healthy, low-cal food from the buffet. Open for breakfast, lunch and dinner.

Top of the Range

Kong Hans
Vingårdsstræde 6
Tel: 33 11 68 68
Located in the old wine cellars of King Hans (1455–1513). One star in the Michelin guide.

Den Sorte Ravn
Nyhavn 14
Tel: 33 13 12 33
The inbaked turbot is the house speciality, but you can't go wrong with anything. Business diners keep coming back.

Restaurationen
Møntergade 19 at Vognmagergade
Tel: 33 14 94 95
The porcelain and candleholders are old but combined in a postmodern way. The chef is young and inspired and the wine selection great.

Something Sweet

La Glace
Skoubogade 3 (off Strøget)
Tel: 33 14 46 46
Sink your teeth into a big, sinful piece of sports-layercake or delicious homemade ice cream in this traditional tea room.

Århus

Mahler
Vestergade 38
Tel: 86 19 06 96
First class food in a French café-style setting. Reservations recommended.

Carlton
Rosensgade 23
Tel: 86 20 21 22
It looks like a café, but it is a trendy restaurant, open from breakfast to midnight. Reservations recommended.

In every street…

Esdragon
Klostergade 6
Tel: 86 12 40 66
The French chef has recreated a charming corner of his homeland here and serves some of the best food in town at moderate prices. Reservations recommended.

Margueritten
Guldsmedgade 20
Tel: 86 19 60 33
Friendly and quiet, with good service and reasonable prices.

…there's service with a smile

Smoked herring

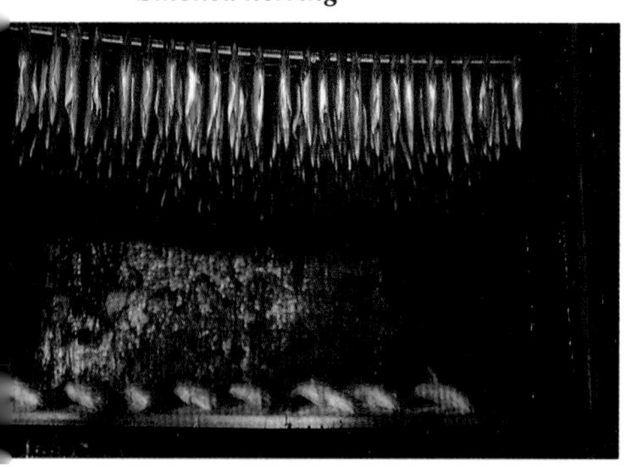

STEDET
Vestergade 60
Tel: 86 19 30 77
Popular, modern restaurant where children will feel welcome.

TEATER BODEGA
Skolegade 7
Tel: 86 12 19 17
Traditional Danish food in a fun bar behind the theatre.

SKOVMØLLEN
At Moesgaard Museum
Tel: 86 27 12 14
A peaceful idyll tucked away in the woods 9km/6 miles south of Århus (bus 6). Wonderful for tea in the afternoon. Closed Monday.

HOUGAARD FRANDSEN
Guldsmedgade at Klostergade
Tel: 86 13 04 00
Wonderful, old-fashioned tea room. Opens for breakfast at 8am.

Don't forget the cafés behind the cathedral. They serve excellent food at prices that are hard to beat.

Skagen

SKAGENS FISKERESTAURANT
On the harbour
Tel: 98 44 35 44
Rough wooden floors and fishing nets on the walls. Don't leave Skagen without stopping by. Reservations recommended.

JECKELS
Jeckelsvej 5
Tel: 98 44 63 00
Lovely, legendary, but expensive restaurant in Gammel Skagen. Reservations recommended.

DE 2 HAVE
Grenen
Tel: 98 44 24 35
The view of the two oceans meeting is the main draw of this, the northernmost restaurant in Denmark. There is also a cafeteria upstairs.

In Skagen, most of the hotels have their own restaurants, eg Clausens Hotel and Hotel Petit. Check the Nightlife chapter for addresses of cafés with dining menus.

Danes prefer healthy food

For up-to-date information about events in Copenhagen, pick up *Neon-Guiden* and *This Week in Copenhagen*. The Friday papers publish listings for the week to come. Ask at the tourist information office or at Use-It (Youth Information Centre) if you can't decipher it.

Cafés

Most cafés are open till 1 or 2am, but a few stay open till 5am.

SOMMERSKO
Kronprinsensgade 6
The first of all the cafés and still one of the liveliest.

DAN TURELL
Store Regnegade 3–5
Thursday–Saturday till 5am.
Run down, but a beloved second home to many art students.

VICTOR
Ny Østergade 8
Upscale restaurant and café.

Nights at Tivoli Gardens

LA BRASSERIE
Hotel d'Angleterre
Kongens Nytorv 34
Upscale café. Subscribes to foreign newspapers.

EUROPA
Amagertorv 1
Nicest café on Strøget, and it sub-

scribes to the *International Herald Tribune*.

Kafé Pår Zalü
Rådhusstræde 13
Downstairs in Huset, with bars and a restaurant upstairs.

Krasnapolsky
Vestergade 10
Large and empty in the morning, crowded and noisy at night.

Sabine
Teglgårdsstræde 4
As local as it can be in the centre of the city.

Dining to music

Park Café
Østerbrogade 79
Somewhat noisy, but always swinging late in the evening.

Bars

Charlie's
Pilestræde 33
Quiet and cozy wine bar.

Palæ 4271
Ny Adelgade 5
The best alternative to the cafés.

Musen & Elefanten
Vestergade 21
The Danish equivalent of an English country pub.

Freud's
Gothersgade 19
Weird drinks and normal people mix well in this bar.

Oxe's Vinbar
Gråbrødre Torv 11
For the young and rich-to-be. Dress code.

The Shamrock Inn
Jernbanegade 9
Popular Irish pub next to Scala.

Alleenberg
Allégade 4
Late night bar for people who like to drink, smoke and talk.

With Live Music

Kafé Rust
Guldbergsgade 8
Good, solid rock from emerging names. Also serves the cheapest meals in town.

Barbue
Rådhusstræde 13
Check out new bands in Huset's rock club.

Bananrepublikken
Nørrebrogade 13
World music disco Thursday and Saturday. Café downstairs, restaurant upstairs. No admission charge, but they raise the prices in the bar during concerts.

Café Pavillionen
Fælledparken
near Nørre Allé & Tagensvej
May–September. Outdoor concerts in

the park. No admission charge, even when big names are playing.

Jazz Bars

JAZZ HOUSE
Niels Hemmingsensgade 10
Modern jazz with lots of ambience.

DE TRE MUSKETERER
Nikolaj Plads
The place to go if you don't like the music at the discos.

MONTMARTRE
Nørregade 41
The oldest jazz club in town, but they book other kinds of bands as well.

VISE VERS HUSET
Bernstorffsgade 7
Listen to ballads and old-fashioned jazz in Tivoli's jazz house.

FINN ZIEGLERS HJØRNE
Vodroffsvej 24
Neighbourhood bar and restaurant owned by a jazz violinist.

Discotheques

The music scene in Copenhagen is so lively that there are few pure discos. Admission charges start at 50kr. Dress up.

AXELS DANSEBAR
Axeltorv 2
Wednesday and Thursday 10pm–3am; Friday and Saturday 11pm–5am. Fastpaced, modern disco with radio DJs.

ANNABEL'S
Lille Kongensgade 16
Wednesday–Saturday 10pm–5am. Smart (and expensive) disco.

EXALON
Frederiksberggade 38
(On Strøget near the town hall square)
Nightly 11pm–6am. Three dance floors with different kinds of music. Very popular.

KRIDTHUSET
Nørregade 1
Monday–Wednesday 7pm–2am; Thursday–Saturday till 5am. Large club for the young crowd.

JAZZ HOUSE
Niels Hemmingsensgade 10
Tuesday–Thursday 8pm–3am; Friday–Saturday 8pm–4pm. When the jazz musicians go home, the dancing crowd comes in.

Classical Music

RADIOHUSETS KONCERTSAL
Julius Thomsensgade 1
Tel: 31 10 16 22 (reservations taken by ARTE)
Concerts with the Radio Big Band and guests.

Ask about concerts in churches at the tourist information office.

Theatres

Most theatres are closed during the summer. You'll get the best information on what's going on in Teaterkiosken (see below).

Det Kongelige Teater
Kongens Nytorv
Tel: 83 14 10 02
Theatre, opera and ballet, September–May. Ask your travel agency for a performance schedule.

Kanonhallen
Serridslevvej 2 (near Park Café)
Tel: 35 43 20 21
Open most of the year. International dance and theatre festivals during the summer.

Teaterkiosken
Fiolstræde at Nørreport Station
Same-night theatre tickets at half price.

Cinemas

All films are shown in the original language with Danish subtitles. Look for listings in the papers. Some locations have cheaper seats on Monday.

Palace
Axel Torv 9
Tel: 33 13 14 00
Several screens in the same building.

Imperial
At Vesterport Station
Tel: 33 11 82 32
Largest screen in Scandinavia.

Grand
Mikkel Bryggersgade 8
Tel: 33 15 16 11
Art films and foreign films.

Park Bio
Østerbrogade 79
Tel: 31 38 33 62
Re-runs at low prices.

Breakfast Places

Café Lee
Linnésgade 16A
Nothing fancy, but when it opens up at 5am, the night crowd comes in.

Hongkong
Nyhavn 7
Old bar in Nyhavn. Open 9am-8am, closes only for a quick clean-up.

Café Sommersko has one of the best brunches in town; they open at 9am (10am Sunday).

Århus

Pick up *Ugen Ud* with listings of live music, art shows, theatre, cinema and more.

Live Music

Bent J.
Nørre Allé 66
Small and cozy jazz bar. Performances usually start at 9pm.

Fatter Eskil
Skolegade 25
Inexpensive restaurant and blues club.

Glazzhuset
Åboulevarden (underneath the pedestrian street)
Large and airy jazz club.

Vestergade 58
Large folk and rock club, named after the address.

Cinema

In Århus, cinema tickets are discounted on Wednesday.

Øst for Paradis
Paradisgade 7–9
Tel: 86 19 31 22
Charming cinema theatre with re-runs.

Skagen

In Skagen, most of the hotels have their own restaurants and bars. Some have live entertainment too, so check out the hotels as you walk by.

ph Musikcafé
Havnevej 16
Restaurant and café with music every night during the summer, followed by disco till 3am.

Café Krøyer
Havneplads 18
Where the Copenhageners meet during the summer.

Fregatten
Trondsvej 20
Sussi and Leo play favourite hits every night. They have become a local attraction.

Skaw Pubben
Havnevej 3
A tiny pub where you can also get some Skagen food to eat.

Atlantic
Havneplads 4
Nightly 11pm–6am.
Discotheque with guest disc jockeys during the summer.

Discotheques

Blitz
Klostergade 34
Nightly 11pm–5am. Three hip-hop-happening floors with live music and a discotheque. Over 21. No admission charge Sunday–Wednesday.

Café Paradis
Paradisgade 7–9
Wednesday–Saturday 11pm–5am. Not a mainstream disco, just take a look at the building. No admission charge Wednesday and Thursday.

Eifel
Store Torv 11
Thursday–Saturday 11am–7am. Rock bar and night-time restaurant.

Classical Music

Music Hall
Thomas Jensens Allé
Tel: 86 13 43 44
Mostly, but not solely, classical concerts.

Ask for a schedule of church concerts at the tourist information office.

Calendar of Special Events

JANUARY/APRIL

There is a reason why these months are not part of the tourist season. The weather is cold, the days are short, and the Danes themselves tend to hide in their homes, where they practise *hygge*, or being cosy. But when the trees start to sprout new leaves and Tivoli opens in late April, things begin to stir.

MAY

The NUMUS New Music Festival in late April or early May is a major event in modern classical music. Composers and musicians from all over Scandinavia meet in Århus to present their works to the public – and to each other.

JUNE

In mid-June, young conductors of classical music compete in the prestigious Malko contest in Copenhagen (Radiohuset).

By the end of the month, Roskilde calls. The rock festival in Roskilde is one of the oldest and largest of the many summer festivals, and it is always a success – even when it rains, as it often does.

Around the same time, there's a festival in Skagen, concentrating on ballads and folk music.

JULY

In early July, the Copenhagen Jazz Festival turns the city upside down with free concerts in the streets and more music in the clubs at night. And when the jazz musicians say goodbye to Copenhagen, some of them head to Århus to meet with other colleagues during the Århus International Jazz Festival in mid-July.

Free (or nearly free) rock concerts sponsored by the breweries have become a summer tradition in Copenhagen. Watch for posters headed *Grøn koncert* and concerts at *Femøren*.

A long, long time ago, people gathered to trade with the Vikings when they came home from their summer expeditions. Moesgaard Museum has revived this tradition (though not the plundering expeditions), and during the last weekend of July you can buy copies of the old produce and eat, drink and have fun with the Vikings.

AUGUST

The Danish National Opera has Wagner on the programme as an introduction to the Århus Festival. Call 86 13 43 44 if you'd like to know more about these marathon performances.

SEPTEMBER

In the second week of September, Århus holds a giant festival. Theatre groups, performance artists and musicians of all kinds flock to the city, and you'd better reserve your hotel room now if you'd like to go the party. Call the Music Hall at 86 13 36 00 for more information.

Meanwhile, Copenhagen hosts a citywide photo festival. In addition to exhibitions, Photo Week sponsors a 24-hour marathon, during which all the participants have to shoot 24 different themes with just one 24-picture roll of film.

OCTOBER

School children have the third week of October off. If you happen to be in Denmark during that week, there will be lots of things to do, but you'll have to share the buses, museums, etc. with lots of kids.

NOVEMBER

As the month separating the autumn vacation from Christmas, November seems to have no separate identity. The wind is not as strong as in October, the mornings not quite as dark as in December. To make things worse, November is just as boring as it is grey.

DECEMBER

Christmas is celebrated on the night of the 24th, but the whole month is filled with Danish *hygge*. The *gløgg* (hot red wine), the fir festoons in the streets, the cakes, the darkness, the candles, the secrets and the sense of expectation give December a charm of its own.

Toy theatre celebrates Xmas

Practical Information

GETTING THERE

Copenhagen: From Kastrup Airport take the SAS bus or the city bus 32 to the city. A taxi from the airport to the city costs around 100 kr.

If you arrive by rail, you might have to get off in Tåstrup. If so, jump on the first train to Københavns Hovedbanegård (the central railway station). Your ticket will be valid for this trip as well.

Århus: The cheapest way to get from Copenhagen (Valby Station) to Århus is by coach. Call 86 78 48 88 for more information. The most comfortable way is by plane to Tirstrup. Take the bus from the airport to Århus or call a taxi on 86 36 34 44 (it's a 45-minute trip). Buses leave from the central train station in Århus 80 minutes before each the departure from Tirstrup Airport.

Skagen: To get to Skagen by train you have to change in Frederikshavn. The nearest airport is in Aalborg, 100km (64 miles) south of Skagen. A ferry connects Skagen with Marstrand in Sweden.

TRAVEL ESSENTIALS

When to Visit

The high season is June, July and August. The weather is sometimes beautiful all summer, and sometimes cold and rainy from the end of June until the beginning of August. Weatherwise, I usually recommend mid-May through mid-June and August as the best times to visit. Then of course, there's Christmas, the peak time for Danish hygge. If you visit out of season, some attractions (like Tivoli) will be closed, but you'll have the museums almost to yourself.

By ferry to Sweden

Visas and Passports

If you are a citizen of Sweden, Norway, Iceland or Finland and arriving from one of those countries, you don't need a passport.

If you are a citizen of Switzerland, Austria or an EC country, you can enter Denmark with certain other identity cards, but you'll have to check with your consulate.

With a few exceptions, everyone else needs at least a passport to enter the country. Citizens of the US, Canada, Australia, New Zealand, Japan, and most other countries do not need visas, but citizens of India, Pakistan or Turkey do. Check with your local Danish consulate before you leave home.

Customs

Denmark has stricter customs regulations than most EC countries. Those regarding liquor and cigarettes are frequently debated and are subject to change. To be safe, don't bring more than one litre of liquor with you, two litres of wine and one carton of cigarettes.

What to Pack

The Danes often wear several layers of clothes: a jacket or sweater above a shirt above a T-shirt, so they can strip off one or more layers as the temperature permits. If you visit during the summer, chances are that you will need both shorts and a sweater. An umbrella might come in handy too. But no matter what you pack, be sure to include some good walking shoes.

Electricity and Time

The voltage is 220V, and you'll be one hour east of Greenwich Mean Time (add one hour to GMT).

GETTING ACQUAINTED

Denmark consists of 406 islands plus the large peninsular of Jutland. It all adds up to about 43,000 sq km (16,600 sq miles) with a coastline of 7,300km (4,500 miles). 5 million people live in the country, ruled by a prime minister and a queen who has only nominal power. Denmark is officially a Lutheran country with a state church. The social security system is one of the best in the world, and the taxes are among the highest.

You'll feel welcome in this orderly little kingdom, where people are usually friendly and eager to help. Just observe these three basic rules: do not litter, do not ignore red lights, and stay happy when you drink.

A view of Danes

MONEY MATTERS

The Danish currency is kroner (crowns), and comes in notes in the denominations of 1,000, 500, 100 and 50 kroner. Coins are 20, 10, 5 and 1 kroner and the smallest are 25 and 50 øre (ears). There are 100 øre in 1 krone.

If you bring travellers cheques, be careful where you cash them. Some banks charge a fee per cheque instead of per transaction, others charge no fee but take a percentage of the amount you exchange, sometimes disguised as a low exchange rate.

Outside banking hours you can change money in the central railway station, 7am–10pm daily (9pm during the winter).

Visa and Master Cards are accepted in most stores, while American Express is less popular. Many restaurants also accept Diners Club cards. If you are in need of cash, look for the bright red cash dispensers called KONTANTEN. They respond to VISA or EuroCheque cards.

Tips and service charges are, in principle, included in all prices. The hairdresser will laugh if you try to tip him, but the maids at the hotel will appreciate that you noticed their good work. So will a waitress in a restaurant and a taxi driver. When you tip, just give a little. Most of the time, 5-20kr. will do.

GETTING AROUND

Denmark has excellent public transport. You won't need a car to follow most of the itineraries in this book, and indeed a car can be troublesome to manoeuvre around in the city. The cities are full of one-way streets, and parking alone will set you back 15 kr. per hour in central Copenhagen. If you bring your own car, you should park it on a side street outside of the parking zones and take the bus or a taxi to the city. The Copenhagen Card will let you ride on all buses and trains in the capital for free, and it will give you access to Tivoli and most of the museums. It is on sale at all tourist information offices and most hotels. Århus has several different kinds of cheap bus tickets for tourists which are also valid for some sightseeing trips.

If you need to rent a car, Østergaard/interRent is one of the best in the business. You'll get good service and fair prices, and the company has offices all around the country:

Copenhagen: Gyldenløvesgade 17. Tel: 33 140 111, Fax: 33 939 029

Århus: Fredensgade 17. Tel: 86 132 133, Fax: 86 199 125

Skagen: at Saga Shipping, Auktionsvej 10. Tel: 98 443 311

The speed limits are 110km/h (70m/h) on motorways, 80km/h (50m/h) on major roads and 50km/h (30m/h) in the city. If you are driving, buy a Marguerit (Daisy) map in a book shop or at a fuel station. It will guide you along all the prettiest country roads.

A bicycle will serve you better than a car on most of the itineraries in this book. The quality of the bikes varies; in Skagen they are in perfect condition and have gears, in Copenhagen they are often below the standard of the bikes you see in the streets. You have to leave a cash deposit, the size of which depends on the condition of the bike.

Copenhagen: Danwheel, Colbjørnsensgade 3. Tel: 31 21 22 27. DSB Cykelcentre in the central train

Trusting to the bus

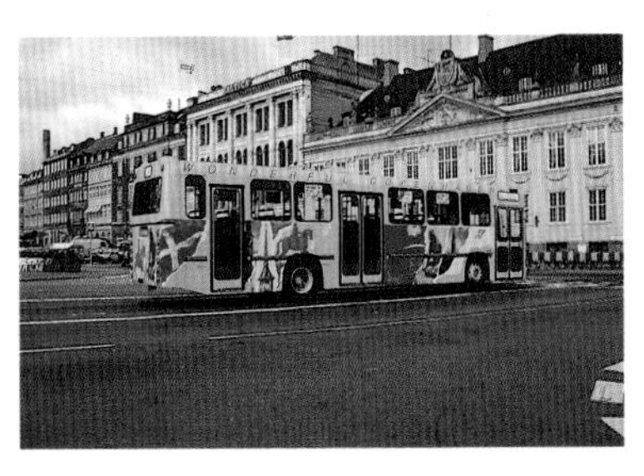

station. Tel: 33 14 07 17 and 33 12 06 07

Århus: Asmussen Cykler, Fredensgade 54. Tel: 86 19 57 00

Skagen: Ahlmann Thomsen next to the train station. Tel: 98 44 12 14

If you are interested in bicycling tours, contact Dansk Cykel Safari, Ny Adelgade 5A (zip code: 1104 København K). Tel: 33 11 11 75

HOURS AND HOLIDAYS

Business Hours

Normal business hours are Monday–Friday 9am–5.30pm and Saturday 9am–1pm. However, bakeries usually open at 6am and non-food shops at 10am. Some supermarkets stay open till 7pm. The first Saturday of the month, most shops stay open until 4 or 5pm, and during the summer every Saturday is considered a 'long' Saturday. In tourist areas, the hours can be even more flexible.

Banks are open Monday–Friday 9.30am–4pm, but Unibank stays open until 5pm. On Thursday, banks and public offices stay open till 6pm.

Public Holidays

1 January, New Year's Day;
Maundy Thursday, Good Friday and Easter Sunday and Monday;
Rogation Day (fifth Sunday after Easter);
Ascension Day (40th Day after Easter – always a Thursday);
Pentecost (seventh Sunday and Monday after Easter);
5 June, Constitution Day. Shops close at noon, banks are closed all day;
24–26 December, Christmas.

WHERE TO STAY

Hotels

Most hotels will put in an extra bed for about a quarter of the cost of a separate room. Some also have group and family specials. Ask for weekend discounts. In Copenhagen most hotels give discounts in July, and in Skagen prices are lower during the winter.

In the listings below, Very Expensive means above 1,200 kr. per night for a double room with shower (breakfast included), Expensive 900–1,200kr., Moderate 600–900kr., Inexpensive 400–600kr., and Cheap below 400kr. You'll get more for your money outside Copenhagen.

Copenhagen

There's a walk-in booking service at the tourist information office in Bernstorffsgade 1. To make reservations in advance, call the hotel directly. Most of the hotels are situated around the central railway station, but another, more luxurious group are clustered around Kongens Nytorv.

D'ANGLETERRE
Kongens Nytorv 34
Tel: 33 12 00 95, Fax: 33 12 11 18
Often rated the best hotel in Copenhagen. You can expect first class service, but will have to pay for it. Very Expensive

HOTEL NEPTUN
Skt. Annæ Plads 14-20
Tel: 33 13 89 00, Fax: 33 14 12 50
Preferred by business travellers, male and female. Conference facilities and a good restaurant, close to Nyhavn. Expensive

Sophie Amalie
Sankt Annæ Plads 21
Tel: 33 13 34 00, Fax: 33 11 77 07
Close to and in the same category as Hotel Neptun. Expensive

Kong Frederik
Vester Voldgade 25-27
Tel: 33 12 59 02
First class hotel close to the town hall, famous for its restaurant. Very Expensive

Josty
Pile Allé 14
Tel: 31 86 90 90, Fax: 38 34 78 50
Nestled in the beautiful park of Frederiksberg Have, this old-fashioned restaurant and hotel is a little out of town, but the birds will sing to you in the morning. Moderate

Ascot Hotel
Studiestræde
Tel: 33 12 60 00, Fax: 33 14 60 40
The beautiful hall of the former Copenhagen Baths serves as the lobby. Moderate to Expensive

Crown Hotel
Vesterbrogade 41
Tel: 31 21 21 66, Fax: 31 21 00 66
Centrally located on busy Vesterbrogade, but no traffic noise. Children are just as welcome as business travellers. Moderate to Expensive

Ibsens Hotel
Vendersgade 23
Tel: 33 13 19 13, Fax: 33 13 19 16
Popular hotel in a quiet street, run by three women. Most rooms have no shower. Moderate

Cab'Inn
Danasvej 32-34
Tel: 31 21 04 00, Fax: 31 21 74 09
If all you need is a nice, clean room the size of a ship cabin and a shower in the morning, try this new concept. With a café downstairs, the Inexpensive Cab'Inn attracts many young travellers.

Århus

Royal Hotel
Store Torv 4
Tel: 86 19 21 22, Fax: 86 19 37 30
Luxury in the centre of town. Inhouse casino. Expensive to Very Expensive

Hotel Ritz
Banegaardspladsen 12
Tel: 86 13 44 44, Fax: 86 13 45 87
Comfortable and centrally located with good service. Inexpensive

Ansgar Missionshotel
Banegaardspladsen 14
Tel: 86 12 41 22, Fax: 86 20 29 04
Nice, clean and somewhat old-fashioned with good service and many single rooms. No alcohol served. Inexpensive

Hotel Mercur
Europaplads
Tel: 86 13 11 11, Fax: 86 13 23 43
Centrally located and modern, but not with much charm. Moderate prices, excellent family and group specials.

Hotel Marselis
Strandvejen 25
Tel: 86 14 44 11, Fax: 86 11 70 46
Every room has an ocean view. 2km/1 mile south of the city. Inexpensive to Moderate

Sømandshjemmet (Sailor's Home)
Havnegade 20
Tel: 86 12 15 99 or 86 12 10 36
Everybody is welcome. Cheap to Inexpensive, with many single rooms.

Hotel La Tour
Randersvej 139
Tel: 86 16 78 88
Motel-like, but nice, north of the city. Inexpensive, special offers if you arrive after 8 without a reservation.

Skagen

To be or to do. That's the question when you visit the tip of Jutland. If you are a doer who would like to see things and go places, you should stay in Skagen. But if you prefer to spend your time on the beach or sipping long drinks in a nice café with an ocean view, then you should go to Højen (=Gammel Skagen) or Kandestederne. Activities there tend to be limited to hiking, swimming, surfing, beachcombing and things related to the sea.

Brøndums Hotel
Anchersvej 3, Skagen
Tel: 98 44 15 55, Fax: 98 45 15 20
A well-known and traditional hotel next to Skagen Museum. Moderate

Hotel Petit
Holstsvej 4, Skagen
Tel: 98 44 11 99, Fax: 98 44 58 50
Just 300m (1,000ft) from the beach, which is as close to it as you can get in Skagen. Moderate

In a romantic city

Clausens Hotel
Sct. Laurentii Vej 35, Skagen
Tel: 98 45 01 66
Centrally located with a nice restaurant. Moderate

Badepension Marienlund
Fabriciusvej 8, Skagen
Tel: 98 44 13 20
Just 12 rooms in a charming old house in Skagen Vesterby. No showers in the rooms. Inexpensive

Skagen Sømandshjem
Østre Strandvej 2, Skagen
Tel: 98 44 21 10, Fax: 98 44 30 28
Hotel for sailors, but others are welcome too. Inexpensive

Ruths Hotel
Hans Ruths Vej 1, Gammel Skagen
Tel: 98 44 11 24, Fax: 98 45 08 75
One of the few hotels in Gammel Skagen that hasn't been turned into timeshare apartments. Moderate to Expensive

Hjorths Hotel
Kandestederne
Tel: 98 48 90 98, Fax: 98 48 78 00
Romantic old hotel, 300m (1,000ft) from the beach. Inexpensive

Kokholms Hotel
Kandestederne
Tel: 98 48 78 00, Fax: 98 48 79 00
Next to Hjorths Hotel and just as pleasant. No single rooms. Moderate

Traditional style

Hotel Skagen Strand
Hulsig
Tel: 98 48 72 22, Fax: 98 48 71 15
Apartments south of Skagen, close to buses and trains. Call for prices.

Niels Skiverens Gaard
Skiveren
Tel: 98 93 22 22
27km (17 miles) south of Skagen, close to the beach and a golf course. Apartments for up to four persons. Moderate

Summerhouses and Apartments

DanCentre
Vibæk Strandvej 12
Tel: 86 34 21 22, Fax: 86 34 48 11
Rents summerhouses all around the country.

Even the city has quiet places

H.A.Y. 4U
Kronprinsensgade 10
Tel: 33 33 08 05, Fax: 33 32 08 04
Rents apartments in the Copenhagen area for a minimum of three days. The company also operates the Royal Hostel (see below).

Bed and Breakfast

Bed and breakfast in Denmark often just means bed and kitchen access. Ask what you get. Rooms cost 100-250kr. depending on the location, or

about half of what the cheapest hotel room will set you back.
In Århus and Skagen, the tourist information office will find a room for you for a nominal fee. In Copenhagen try one of these:

Bed and Breakfast
Amagertorv 9 mezz
DK–1160 Copenhagen K
Tel: 33 32 92 33

Skandinavisk Logi and Morgenmad
St. Kongensgade 94
DK–1264 Copenhagen K
Tel: 33 91 91 15, Fax: 33 91 91 85

Dansk Bed and Breakfast
Postbox 53
Hesselvang 20
DK–2900 Hellerup
Write to the company for a brochure, then call the B&B places directly.

Youth Hostels and Sleep-Ins

Copenhagen

The Royal Hostel
Kronprinsensgade 10, 1st floor
Tel: 33 33 08 05, Fax: 33 32 08 04
Wonderful little hostel in the centre of the city. Call to make reservations, then post a deposit.

Århus

Brobjergskolen Sleep-In
Frederiksallé 20
A school building used as sleep-in,

mid-June–September. Open 24hrs, no advance booking. Some family rooms.

Skagen

DANHOSTEL GAMMEL SKAGEN
Højensvej 32
Tel: 98 44 13 56

Camping

You have to stay on an authorised campground – camping in the fields etc. is prohibited by law.

Copenhagen: The campground closest to the city lies in BELLAHØJ at Hvidkildevej, tel: 31 10 11 50, open May 31–August 31 (bus 13 to town). But the nicest is STRANDMØLLEN CAMPING north of the city at Strandmøllevej 2 in Klampenborg, tel: 42 80 38 83, open May 15–August 31 (train to the city from Skodsborg Station). ABSALON CAMPING in Rødovre at Korsdalsvej 132, tel: 31 41 06 00 is open all year round.

Århus: The nicest place to camp is BLOMMEHAVEN 4km (2½ miles) south of the city (take bus 6 or 19). It is situated by the sea in Marselisborg woods and open mid-April–mid-September. Make reservations on tel: 86 27 02 07, fax: 86 14 25 99.

Skagen: There are several campgrounds around Skagen, all of them very popular. You have to make reservations in advance! Check with a camping guide or try GRENEN CAMPING just north of the city, Fyrvej 16, tel: 98 44 25 46.

EATING OUT

The international influence on the Danish cuisine has made the menus easier to decode in recent years. But when it comes to traditional Danish dishes, you'll need assistance. These are the basics, but don't hesitate to ask the waiter.

Morgenmad	Breakfast
Frokost	Lunch
Middag	Dinner
Smørrebrød	Open face sandwiches
Rugbrød	Black (rye) bread
Franskbrød	White (wheat) bread
Flûte	Crusty white bread
Bolle	Roll
Pålæg	Cold cuts
Sild	(Pickled) herring
Tartar	Steak tartar
Leverpostej	Liver paté
Ost	Cheese
Fisk and *Skaldyr*	Fish and Shellfish
Fiskefilet	Fillet of fish
Rødspætte	Plaice
Forel	Trout
Tun	Tuna
(Røget) laks	(Smoked) salmon
Stjerneskud	Fillet of fish with shrimp and asparagus
Rejer	Prawns
Fjordrejer	Freshwater shrimps
Muslinger	Mussels
Hummer	Lobster
Grøntsager	Vegetables
Kartofler	Potatoes
Løg	Onion
Champignon	Mushrooms
Bønner	Beans
Gulerod	Carrot
Majs	Corn
Kål	Cabbage
Salat	Lettuce/Salad
Tomat	Tomato
Agurk	Cucumber

Hovedretter	*Entrées*
Flæskesteg	Pork roast
Frikadelier	Meat balls
Mørbradbøf	Tenderloin (often cooked in a sauce)
Bøf	Steak
Hakkebøf	Burger
Kylling	Chicken
Kalkun	Turkey
And	Duck
Desserter	Desserts
Pandekager	Pancakes
Lagkage	Layercake
Småkage	Cookies
Kransekage	Marzipan stick
Wienerbrød	Pastry
Is, sorbet	Ice cream, sherbet ice

EMERGENCIES

In case of fire or accident dial 112. Emergency calls are free.

Medical Services

Check the agreements on medical coverage with the authorities or health insurance in your home country, preferably before you leave. Doctors will usually ask to be paid in cash, but you might be able to get some of the amount refunded. If you have to go to the hospital due to sudden illness, treatment is free. To find the nearest casualty ward, dial information on 118.

Copenhagen: Dial 33 93 63 00 to get a doctor on call, Monday–Friday 8am–4pm. At night, call 33 12 00 41 in the city centre, Østerbro and Nørrebro, 31 10 00 41 at Frederiksberg, and 31 22 00 41 at Vesterbro and Valby.

Århus: Call 86 20 10 22, 4pm–8am and weekends.

Skagen: Monday–Friday 8am–4pm, dial 98 44 13 96, other hours 98 43 36 22.

Pharmacies

Copenhagen: Steno Apotek, Vesterbrogade 6C across from the central train station, tel: 33 14 82 66; 24hrs, service charge after normal business hours.

Århus: Løve Apoteket, Store Torv 5, tel: 86 12 00 22, 24hrs with service charge.

Skagen: Sct. Laurentii Vej 44, tel: 98 44 17 58.

Dentists

Copenhagen: Tandlægevagten, Oslo Plads 14; daily 8–9.30pm, Saturday–Sunday also 10am–noon.

Århus: Mr. Sahlertz, tel: 85 15 73 11, daily 8–9pm, Sunday also 9–10am.

Skagen: Call 98 44 28 70 or ask at the tourist information office.

Other Emergencies

You don't have to be overly concerned about your personal safety during your visit. Even at night, the cities are generally safe. But during the summer pickpockets flock to the tourist areas, especially to Copenhagen. Be careful never to leave your purse or jacket out of sight, not even in the hotel. In particular be alert if several people try to get your attention at the same time, and keep your money and belongings as close to your body as you can.

Should you lose your MasterCard, VISA, Eurocard or EuroCheques, call 44 89 25 00 (24hrs). If you lose your American Express card, call 80 01 00 21 straight away.

Copenhagen: The lost property office lies in Vanløse at Slotsherrensvej 113 (next to Islev S-train station), tel: 31 74 88 221. Hours are 9am–2pm, Thursday to 5pm, closed Saturday and Sunday. If you lose something on the bus, call 36 45 45 45, Monday–Friday 10am–5pm. If you lose something on the train, call 36 44 20 10, same hours. If you need to get in touch with the police, ask around for the nearest police station, or go to Nyropsgade 20 between Vesterport Station and the lakes, tel: 31 91 14 48.

Århus: The police station is located at Ridderstræde 1, tel: 86 13 30 00.

Skagen: The police station is located at Rolighedsvej, tel: 98 44 14 44.

COMMUNICATIONS AND MEDIA

Telephone

The country code for Denmark is 45.

To call foreign countries direct, dial 009 + country code + area code + number.

To reach the operator, dial 113, for information 118.

You can charge calls to the US on an AT&T card if you dial 800-10010 (do not dial 009-1 first), to a SPRINT card on 800-10877 and to other credit cards on 800-10022. Key country codes are: Australia (61); Germany (49); Italy (39); Japan (81); The Netherlands (31); Spain (34); United Kingdom (44); United States and Canada (1).

To call from a public phone booth, lift the receiver, place coins in the groove on the top and dial the number you want.

Emergency calls are free (dial 112).

Post Offices

Copenhagen: Købmagergade 33, Tel: 33 32 12 12. Monday-Friday 9am–6pm, Saturday 9am–1pm; The Central Railway Station, Monday–Friday 8am–10pm, Saturday 9am–4pm, Sunday 10am–5pm.

Århus: Banegaardspladsen 14, Tel: 86 13 13 33. Monday–Friday 9am–5.30pm, Saturday 9am–noon.

Skagen: Christian X's Vej 8, Tel: 98 44 23 44. Monday–Friday 9.30am–5pm, Saturday 9.30am–noon.

Media

You can get news in English on the radio (90.9MHz) Monday–Friday at 8.10am.

USEFUL INFORMATION

For the Disabled

An inexpensive brochure is available from the Danish tourist association, with information on accommodation, transportation and sights with wheelchair access. The Danish Handicap Association (Hans Knudsens Plads 1A 1st floor, 2100 Copenhagen Ø, Tel: 31 29 35 55) can also help you.

For Gay Visitors

The gay and lesbian society, Foreningen af 1948, operates two discotheques and cafés called Pan Club: Knabrostræde 3 in Copenhagen, tel: 33 13 19 48, and Jægergårdsgade 42 in Århus, tel: 86 13 43 80.

Babysitting

Studenternes Babysitting has been in business for 40 years and still operates at modest rates. Call well in advance on 31 22 96 96, 6.30–9am (winter only) or 3–6pm.

Bookshops

Boghallen, Politikens Hus
Rådhuspladsen 35, Cph.
Tel: 33 11 85 11
Large selection of books in English.

Steve's Books and Records
Ved Stranden 10, Cph.
Tel: 33 11 94 60
Specialises in jazz literature and records.

G.E.C. Gad
Vimmelskaftet 32, Cph.
Tel: 33 15 05 58
Outlets in several cities.

The British Book Shop
Badstuestræde 8, Cph.
Tel: 33 93 11 15

Biblioteksboghandelen
Kultorvet 2, Cph.
Tel: 33 13 25 27
Large selection of souvenir books.

Kristian F Møller
Store Torv 5, Århus
Tel: 86 13 06 99, Fax: 86 13 09 06
The best book shop in Århus.

Attractions

Below is a listing of museums and sights that didn't fit into any of the itineraries, but are nevertheless worth a visit. Bus 388 (from Lyngby Station to Helsingør Station) passes by both Ordrupgaard, Rungstedlund and Nivågård.

Copenhagen

Tycho Brahe Planetarium
Gammel Kongevej on Lake Sankt Jørgen
Tel: 33 12 12 24
Tuesday–Thursday 8.30am–9pm, Friday–Monday 10.30am–9pm
Large and modern planetarium with Omnimax theatre. The admission charge varies from 10–110kr. depending on what you'd like to see.

Thorvaldsens Museum
Porthusgade 2
Tel: 33 32 15 32
Tuesday–Sunday 10am–5pm
The works and collections of Danish sculptor Bertel Thorvaldsen (1770–1844) in a beautiful building next to Christiansborg.

The Planetarium

Davids Samling
Kronprinsessegade 30
Tel: 33 13 55 64
Tuesday–Sunday 1–4pm
A fine collection of Islamic art and European applied arts from the 18th century. Free

The Toy Museum
Valkendorffsgade 13
Tel: 33 14 10 09
Monday–Thursday 9am–4pm, Saturday–Sunday: 10am–4pm, Friday closed
The history of toys presented through toy landscapes. Adults 22kr., children 12kr.

Ordrupgaard
Vilvordevej 110, Charlottenlund
Tel: 31 64 11 83
Tuesday–Sunday 1–5pm
Paintings by French impressionists and Danish 19th-century painters. Adults 20kr., children free.

The Karen Blixen Museum
Rungstedlund
Rungsted Strandvej 111
Tel: 42 57 10 57
May–September: daily 10am–5pm
October–April: Wednesday–Friday 1–4pm, Saturday–Sunday 11am–4pm
The home of Karen Blixen (Isak Dinesen), author of *Out of Africa*. Adults 30kr., children free.

Nivågård Art Collection
Gammel Strandvej 2
Tel: 42 24 10 17
15th–19th century paintings from the Netherlands, Italy and Denmark. Adults 25kr., children free.

Århus

Moesgaard Museum of Prehistory
Moesgaard Allé 20
Tel: 86 27 24 33
April–October: daily 10am–5pm; January–March and November–December: Tuesday–Sunday 10am–4pm
Denmark's history from the Stone Age to the Viking era. Situated in the woods near the beach (take bus 6). Viking Meet the last weekend of July. Adults 25kr., children free.

Tivoli Friheden
Skovbrynet
Tel: 86 14 73 00
May: 1–10pm, June–August: 1–11pm
Amusement park south of the city. Take bus 4. Adults 22kr., children 10kr.

The Women's Museum
Domkirkeplads 5 (behind the Cathedral)
Tel: 86 13 61 44
June–mid-September: daily 10am–5pm; January–May and mid-September–December: Tuesday–Sunday 10am–4pm
A small museum dedicated to the modern history of women. Adults 10kr., children 5kr.

In the Toy Museum

LEGOLAND
Billund in mid-west Jutland
Tel: 75 33 13 33
May–mid-September: 10am–8pm
The famous park full of miniature landscapes built entirely of Lego bricks. Take a Centrum Turist tour (Tel: 86 19 00 00) from Århus or buy a special Legoland ticket at the train station.

Skagen

EAGLE WORLD
On the road to Hirtshals
Tel: 98 93 20 31
April–September
Eagles and falcons live in the wild out here, but you can still get close to them. Visitors are let in only at 9–10am and 4–5pm. Call in advance to check times.

LANGUAGE

Danish spelling is somewhat arbitrary. Most vowels have more than one pronunciation (like the English 'i' in 'win' and 'wine'), and you can't always tell from the spelling which one to use. Just to make it all the more confusing, Danish also makes frequent use of a glottal stop, which is not reflected in the spelling, plus three or four more vowels than most languages. And then there's the question of dialects. So don't expect to become fluent in a month. Luckily, most Danes speak English and will be happy to volunteer their assistance when you need it. You can get a long way with German too.

But if you'd still like to try to make sense of street signs and the like, these are the basic rules for pronunciation:

a – a, as in 'cat'or as in French 'la'
e – as in 'bed' or, as an ending vowel, just like ø
i – ee as in 'sleep'
o – as in 'more' or just like å
u – u, as in 'put'
y – say 'ee' while you round your lips
æ – as in 'bear'
ø – as in 'fur' or say æ while you round your lips
å – aw, as in 'paw'

Days of the Week

Mandag (Monday), *tirsdag*, *onsdag*, *torsdag*, *fredag*, *lørdag*, *søndag*.

Months of the Year

Januar (January), *februar*, *marts*, *april*, *maj*, *juni*, *juli*, *august*, *september*, *oktober*, *november*, *december*.

The 24th of January 1993 is written: *24. januar 1993* or *24.1.1993*

Numbers

1	*en/et*
2	*to*
3	*tre*
4	*fire*
5	*fem*
6	*seks*
7	*syv*
8	*otte*
9	*ni*
10	*ti*
11	*elleve*
12	*tolv*
13	*tretten*
14	*fjorten*
15	*femten*
16	*seksten*
17	*sytten*
18	*atten*
19	*nitten*
20	*tyve*
21	*en-og-tyve*
22	*toogtyve*
23	*treogtyve*
30	*tredive*
40	*fyrre*
50	*halvtreds*
60	*tres*
70	*halvfjerds*
80	*firs*
90	*halvfems*
100	*hundrede*
200	*tohundrede*
300	*trehundrede*
1000	*tusind*
2000	*totusind*
12.345	*tolvtusind-trehundrede-femogfyrre*

Words and Phrases

goddag	hello
farvel	good-bye
hej	(replaces both the above)
godmorgen	good morning
godnat	good night
ja, jo	yes
nej	no
tak	thank you
ja tak	yes, please
nej tak	no, thanks
gade	road
vej	way
sti	trail
allé	avenue
plads or *torv*	square
gård	courtyard
have	garden
ingen adgang	no admittance
må ikke berøres	do not touch
tilladt	allowed
forbudt	forbidden
gratis	free
værelser	rooms
med bad	with shower
udsigt	view
etage or *sal*	floor

The ground floor is called *stuen*. First floor is the floor above *stuen*.

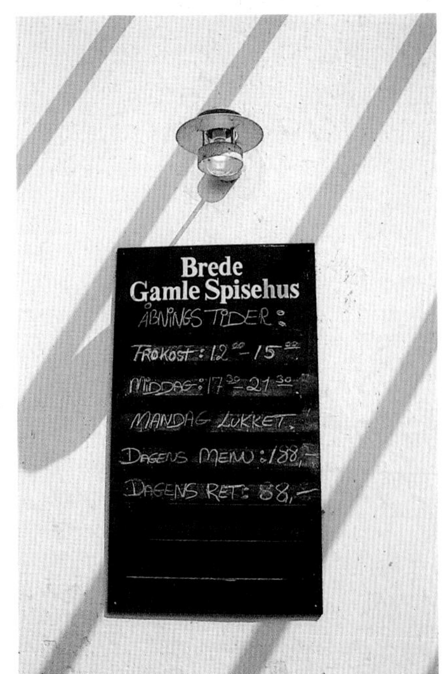

nord, nordre	north, northern
syd, søndre	south, southern
øst, østre	east, eastern
vest, vestre	west, western
gammel	old
ny	new

'Please' does not correspond to one word or phrase, but is expressed in the construction of the sentence. Danes will often forget to say 'please' in English, but have no intention of being rude.

SPORT

Copenhagen This Week has extensive listings of bowling and badminton halls, boat rental companies and much more. In Århus and Skagen, look for local posters.

Spectator Sports

Ask the local tourist information office to assist you in finding and buying tickets.

Swimming

There is easy access to good white sand beaches just about anywhere in the country. A blue flag denotes that the beach is clean and the water clear. Swimming can occasionally be dangerous, especially on the west coast. Use common sense, and stay out of the water whenever the red flag is flying. On the west coast, climbing the dunes can be dangerous, and it is strictly prohibited.

Sailing, Canoeing and Waterskiing

FOSS CHARTERS
Vibevænget 7, Beder at Århus
Tel: 30 86 10 65, 86 93 20 65
Diving, waterskiing and sightseeing tours.

KALØVIG BÅDEHAVN
Tel: 86 99 19 67, Fax: 86 99 45 38
Boat rental in Skødstrup north of Århus.

MOESGAARD STRAND KIOSK
Boat rental, take bus No 19 from Århus to Moesgaard Strand.

Fishing

There are good opportunities in virtually every area of the country, but you must obtain a local fishing licence before you go out. Ask the tourist information office to assist you. In Skagen, you can take 1–3 day ocean tours with:

SKAGEN MARINE CENTRE
Kvasevej 4
Tel: 98 44 13 88

Horseback Riding

MOESGAARD STRAND, ÅRHUS
Tel: 86 22 55 44
Weekdays 10am–2pm
Guided tours through the woods, June–August. Take bus 19.

VILHELMSBORG MANOR HOUSE
Bedervej 101, Mårslet at Århus
Tel: 86 93 71 11, Fax: 86 93 74 72
Manor house turned into an equestrian centre. Call to get a schedule of classes and events.

USEFUL ADDRESSES

Tourist Offices

Copenhagen: Bernstorffsgade 1 (between Tivoli and the train station), tel: 33 11 13 25

Use-It (Youth Information Centre), Rådhusstræde 13, Tel: 33 15 65 18

Århus: The Town Hall, tel: 86 12 16 00, Fax: 86 12 08 07

Skagen: Sct. Laurentii Vej 22, tel: 98 44 13 77

FURTHER READING

Background Reading

An Outline History of Denmark, by Helge Seidelin Jacobsen, Høst and Søn, 1990.

Facts about Denmark, Ministry of Foreign Affairs, frequent updates.

Signposts to Denmark, by Anne Warburton (former British ambassador to Denmark), Hernov, 1992.

Guide Books

Insight Guide: Denmark, Apa Publications, 1991.

Tivoli – The Magic Garden, by Ebbe Mørk, Høst and Søn, 1988.

On a Tour to Nordsjælland, by Ole Schierbeck, Høst and Søn, 1989.

Camping Danmark, in Danish, German and English. The Camping Council, annual updates.

Café – The Café Guide to Copenhagen, Per Kofoed, 1992.

Souvenir Books

Hans Christian Andersen's Denmark, Rhodos, 1983.

Copenhagen – Open Spaces and *Copenhagen – Interiors*, by Peder Olesen, Borgen, 1991.

Green Denmark, by Anders Tvevad, Skarv•Høst and Søn, 1992.

Denmark, by Sven Skovmand and Henrik Saxgren, Hedeskov, 1988.

Denmark, by Søren Lauridsen, Mathilde, 1991.

A

B

C

H

I, J

K

L

M

N, O

P

R

Art & Photo Credits

Photography by **Marianne Paul** *and*
Pages 6/7, 16T, 18, 21T, 22T, 23, 29T, 46T, 46B, 68, 71, 72, 86 **Danish Tourist Board**
12 **Bert Wiklund**
16B, 73 **Topham Picture Source**

Production Editor **Erich Meyer**
Handwriting **V. Barl**
Cartography **Berndtson & Berndtson**

NOTES